Cricket as a Catalyst for Social Change in India

Cricket as a Catalyst for Social Change in India

Rafeal Mechlore

Leader Enterprises

CONTENTS

INDEX

Introduction

1. The significance of cricket in India
2. Historical context of cricket in India
3. Overview of the book's purpose and structure

INTRODUCTION

In the context of India, cricket is much more than just a sport; it is a force that is powerful and pervasive that has knitted itself into the very fabric of the nation. Cricket in India is a cultural phenomenon that resonates far beyond the bounds of the playing field. With millions of enthusiastic supporters and an intricate history stretching back to the colonial era, cricket in India has a history that dates back to the British rule. It is a spectacle that has the ability to captivate the nation, delivering moments of pride, passion, and solidarity, and it has emerged as a driver for significant societal change. This book, titled "Cricket as a Catalyst for Social Change in India," delves into the multifaceted role that cricket plays in shaping the social dynamics of the country. The author examines cricket's historical evolution, impact on identity, gender equality, caste dynamics, regional unity, education, philanthropy, and the challenges that it faces.

One must first comprehend the historical setting of cricket before being able to comprehend the deeply ingrained influence that it has in India. Cricket was brought to the Indian subcontinent by the British colonial administration. Over the course of its history there, it transitioned from being a pastime popular among the colonists to a sport that resonated deeply with the Indian populace. In spite of linguistic, cultural, and regional disparities, the sport started to become a reflection of, and contributor to, the national identity. Cricket evolved as a means by which Indians could assert their identity, and it went on to play an essential part, over the course of several decades, in developing a sense of oneness among an otherwise heterogeneous society. Whether it was India's maiden Test triumph against England in 1952 or the famous win of the 1983 World Cup, iconic moments on the cricket field are carved into the collective consciousness of the nation. One such moment was the win of the 1983 World Cup. These examples illustrate how cricket has not only been a reflection of India's identity but also a medium through which Indians may communicate their sense of pride in their country.

The advancement of gender equality in India is one of the most astounding changes that can be attributed to the sport of cricket's widespread popularity there. In spite of the fact that cricket has traditionally been thought of as a male-dominated sport, the development of women's cricket as a serious and respected equivalent has been a ground-breaking movement in recent years. Female cricketers have smashed preconceptions, encouraging young girls and defying conventional views about the roles that should be played by men and women. This book will examine the extraordinary journeys of female cricketers who have defied cultural expectations and will emphasize their accomplishments as well as their contributions to the movement toward the elimination of gender barriers. In addition to this, it investigates the role that women's cricket has had in shifting gender roles in India, with the goal of promoting self-determination and equality between the sexes.

In addition to this, cricket has tackled and challenged the deeply rooted caste relations that exist in India. Cricket has opened doors of opportunity for those from underprivileged castes, allowing them to break free from the constraints of societal discrimination and ascend to prominent positions in the sport. The sport of cricket has evolved into a platform for social mobility and inclusivity, as seen by the uplifting stories of cricket players who came from homes considered to be lower caste. This book will dive into these stories of perseverance and talent, as well as the transforming impact of cricket in overcoming discrimination based on caste. In addition to this, it will investigate the activities and policies within the ecosystem of cricketing that try to promote inclusivity and diversity in order to guarantee that the game continues to provide an equal playing field for all participants.

Another important way in which cricket has had a big impact on Indian society is through the phenomenon of regionalism. Cricket is both a uniting and a dividing force, despite its ability to accentuate the rivalries that exist between different regions. The Indian Premier League (IPL) is a prime example of how cricket can develop a sense of national belonging while simultaneously honoring a sense of regional pride. This book examines how the Indian Premier League (IPL), which features city-based franchises, has not only altered the competitive environment of cricket but has also become a celebration of the rich cultural diversity of India. Cricket fans all around the country feel closer to one another thanks to the healthy competition that exists between their respective cities and states. At the same time, this healthy competition contributes to the ever-increasing interest in the sport.

In India, the sport of cricket and education have grown inextricably intertwined. Many young people who are interested in playing cricket see it as a potential method to improve their lives in the years to come. The proliferation of scholarship programs, cricket academies, and coaching facilities across the country gives gifted youngsters the opportunity to perfect their abilities and secure a bright scholastic future for themselves. This book investigates the ways in which cricket has impacted educational goals, inspiring a generation of young athletes to pursue their ambitions with the knowledge that cricket can serve as a springboard for both their personal and their societal development.

In addition to this, cricket has developed into a forum for charitable activities and community service projects. Cricketers, cricket teams, and cricket organizations have all been actively involved in charitable activity, making use of their power and resources to address social concerns and give back to the communities in which they live. This book focuses on significant examples of cricketers who have committed themselves to social concerns, and it sheds light on how these efforts have made a meaningful difference in the lives of countless persons all across India. In addition to this, it highlights the social responsibility activities performed by cricket organizations and the effects those initiatives have had on a variety of communities.

In spite of the numerous positive aspects of the sport, cricket in India has not been spared from difficulties and debates. The game has had its fair share of moral conundrums, the most notable of which were the match-fixing scandals that shook the cricketing world. In addition, the integrity of the game has been tainted by instances of corruption as well as power battles within the administration of cricket. This book dives deep into these topics, investigating the influence such problems have had on the image of the sport, as well as the steps that have been made to remedy these difficulties. This article explores the moral conundrums and ethical challenges that cricket must address in order to bring about social transformation.

This book takes a forward-looking approach by investigating the developing tendencies and innovations in Indian cricket that have the potential to create additional social transformation. The sport is primed for continuing development as a result of a number of factors, including the impact of technology and data analytics as well as the expanding reach of cricket thanks to digital platforms.

"Cricket as a Catalyst for Social Change in India" is an in-depth investigation of how cricket, beyond its position as a sport, has significantly altered the social dynamics of India. The title of this investigation is "Cricket as a Catalyst for Social Change in India." It is a voyage through time that traces the historical growth of cricket in India, its role in building national identity, its influence on gender equality, caste dynamics, regional unity, education, and philanthropy, as well as its confrontations with problems and controversies. This is a book that takes the reader on a journey through time. This book tries to provide a comprehensive understanding of how a sport can be a catalyst for social change, reflecting and altering the dynamically diversified environment of India in the process. This narrative is a monument to the continuing power of cricket to bring people together, inspire innovation, and propel change in the democracy with the largest population in the world.

1. **The significance of cricket in India**

   In India, cricket is more than simply a sport; it is also a way of life, a religion, a unifying force, and a wellspring of untamed enthusiasm. Cricket, which has a long and illustrious history and is played by passionate fans, has a place that is one of a kind and unmatched in the Indian subcontinent, which is home to a diverse and culturally rich tapestry. In this essay, we will investigate the deep-seated significance of cricket in India, touching on its historical development, as well as its social influence, economic repercussions, and place as a cultural emblem.

The Origins in History:

The British colonial government is credited with bringing cricket to the Indian subcontinent in the 18th century, marking the beginning of the sport's long history in India. The first known game of cricket was played in India in the year 1721, and the sport steadily acquired popularity among the British expatriates and the Indian elites over the following decades. The formation of cricket clubs and associations allowed the sport to become more accessible to people of a wider range of backgrounds within India.

Cricket, on the other hand, didn't start making significant inroads into Indian society until the

latter half of the 19th century. The Parsi community was the first to take an interest in the sport and begin playing it, which was quickly followed by other communities. In the year 1848, the city of Bombay, which is today known as Mumbai, became home to the first Indian cricket club: the Oriental Cricket Club. This event marked the beginning of the change from a sport that was dominated by British participants to one that welcomed participants from India. A major turning point in the progression of cricket in India was the establishment of the Board of Control for Cricket in India (BCCI) in 1928. This event is referred to as "the BCCI." The Board of Control for Cricket in India (BCCI) was established as the governing authority for cricket in the country, with responsibility for the growth, administration, and organization of the sport. During this time period, India competed against England in their first Test match, which took place in 1932.

Pride in One's Identity and Country:

In India, cricket has gone far beyond its roots as a sport and evolved into a representation of the country's unique culture. The success of the Indian cricket team has frequently been a source of national pride and has served as a unifying element in India, which is noted for the linguistic, cultural, and regional variety that exists inside its borders. Iconic milestones in the history of cricket have left an everlasting impact on the collective consciousness of the nation, such as India's maiden Test series triumph in 1952 against England and the historic win of the World Cup in 1983.

Legends of Indian cricket such as Kapil Dev, Sachin Tendulkar, and Virat Kohli have entered the public consciousness and are admired not only for their abilities as cricket players but also for the way in which they exemplify the spirit and aspirations of the Indian people. Cricket matches, particularly those played against arch-rivals Pakistan, are known to elicit tremendous feelings and a sense of national pride throughout the country. The sport is frequently utilized by Indians as a medium through which they are able to convey their sense of national pride.

Implications for the Economy:

It is impossible to overstate the positive impact that cricket has had on India's economy. Since its inception in 2008, the Indian Premier League (IPL) has brought about a sea change in the way cricket is played and profited from in India. In addition to being a spectacular display of cricket, the Indian Premier League is also a massively successful business venture. It boasts an impressive roster of performers, is attended by athletes from around the world, and secures massive television and sponsorship deals.

Because it is based on a franchise system, the Indian Premier League (IPL) has become one of the most lucrative leagues in the world. It has been a crucial factor in the expansion of the Indian economy, as it has resulted in the generation of a huge amount of cash from the sale of tickets, goods, advertising, and broadcasting rights. As a result of the Indian Premier League, several ancillary sectors such as sports marketing, event management, and the entertainment industry have emerged, further contributing to the expansion of the economy.

In addition, the economic significance of cricket reaches all the way down to grassroots development. The possibility of amassing wealth motivates a great number of young people who come from less privileged circumstances to pursue a career in the sport of cricket. Cricket academies, coaching centers, and talent scouting have all developed into thriving enterprises that contribute to the expansion of the entire economy and the creation of new jobs.

Influence on Society:

Cricket has been a significant contributor to the social transformation that has taken place in India. The movement toward gender equality is one of the most significant shifts that has taken place in recent history. Although cricket has always been thought of as a male-dominated sport, the development of women's cricket as a respectable alternative has been a ground-breaking shift in perception in recent years. Female cricketers have smashed preconceptions, encouraging young girls and defying conventional views about the roles that should be played by men and women. The accomplishments of the Indian women's cricket team, particularly in the most recent years, have had a constructive effect on cultural attitudes around gender roles and have made a significant contribution to the advancement of women's rights in their nation.

Cricket has also presented a challenge to the caste hierarchies that are strongly embedded in Indian society. The activity has opened doors for people from underprivileged backgrounds, allowing them to emerge as leaders in their fields and triumph over the restrictions imposed by discriminatory social norms. The sport of cricket has evolved into a platform for social mobility and inclusivity, as seen by the uplifting stories of cricket players who came from homes considered to be lower caste. Within the ecosystem of cricket, there are initiatives and policies that strive to promote diversity and ensure that the sport continues to provide an equal playing field for all participants.

In addition, cricket has evolved into a platform for the discussion of social issues as well as charitable giving. Cricketers, cricket teams, and cricket organizations have all been actively involved in philanthropic work, utilizing their power and resources to give back to the areas in which they live. The fact that these initiatives have produced a discernible improvement in the lives of countless people all over India demonstrates the significant role that sports can play in the promotion of social responsibility.

Symbol of Cultural Identity:

The game of cricket is strongly rooted in the social and cultural traditions of India. Not only does it have a place on the field, but it also has a position in the world of literature, art, music, and film. The lingo and metaphors associated with cricket are smoothly integrated into ordinary discussion. In many Indian homes, the televisions are usually tuned to cricket broadcasts, thus the roar of the crowd can be heard in the background.

Cricket is more than just a sport; it's also a way to pass the time with friends, a fun way to meet new people, and a great way to strengthen relationships. Families, friends, and acquaintances get together to watch matches together, and they rejoice over victory and commiserate over losses as a group. The cricket stadium is a location where emotions run strong, and the passion of the crowd is contagious; examples include Kolkata's traditional Eden Gardens and Mumbai's modern Wankhede Stadium.

The Cricket World Cup, the Twenty20 World Cup, and the Indian Premier League have all evolved into massive cultural festivities that include music, dance, and pyrotechnics in addition to their traditional roles as international athletic competitions. The Indian diaspora might feel a stronger feeling of connection to their homeland through the sport of cricket, which is one reason why they consider it to be an essential component of their cultural identity.

Cricket is a lively and intricate thread that can be found woven throughout the social fabric, cultural fabric, and economic landscape of India. It has been elevated to the rank of a national institution due to the fact that it has historical roots, is of national significance, has economic ramifications, and has a transformative social influence. Cricket is more than just a sport; it is a mirror of India's variety, a source of solidarity, a vehicle for social change, and a cultural emblem that is widely recognized throughout the entirety of the country. Cricket is a timeless and enduring force that continues to bring people together, bind them in their love for the game, and display the unlimited possibilities of passion and togetherness in India, despite the fact that India is constantly changing and developing.

2. **Historical context of cricket in India**

Cricket is more than simply a sport in India; it is also a cultural phenomenon that has a long, illustrious history that spans over two centuries. This history is both rich and complex. The history of cricket in India is a reflection of the evolving political, social, and cultural milieu of India as a whole. In this essay, we will look into the historical backdrop of cricket in India, tracing its roots all the way back to the colonial era and continuing all the way up to the present day.

Origins in Colonial Times:

During the time that India was under British colonial rule, the sport of cricket was first played there. The first known game of cricket to be played on Indian land took place in 1721 at Cambay, Gujarat, between British sailors and local inhabitants. The game was played against each other. However, during its formative years, cricket was primarily a sport played by members of the British upper class as well as expatriates. In India, the game was almost entirely confined to the clubs and grounds that were owned by the British, and Indians had very restricted access to it.

The development of cricket as a sport in India was greatly aided by the formation of many associations and clubs dedicated to the game. One of the earliest cricket clubs in the subcontinent, the Calcutta Cricket Club dates back to 1792 when it was established. These clubs were instrumental in establishing the early rules of the game and spreading its popularity, playing a key role in both of these areas.

In the year 1848, the Oriental Cricket Club was established in Bombay, which is today known as Mumbai. This event marked a significant turning point as Indians started to enjoy the sport. This club, which was established by members of the Parsi community, marked the beginning of the change from cricket being played only by British players to cricket being played by Indian players. The participation of the Parsis in cricket is generally seen as the starting point of a more widespread Indian interest in the game.

The First Cricket Team to Represent India:

Because of the Parsis' passion for the game of cricket, India sent its first cricket team to play in England for the very first time. A group of Parsi cricketers, commanded by Sorabji Pochkhanawala, set sail for England in 1886 to take part in a historic tour of the country. The tour was an important landmark in the annals of Indian cricket history. It served as a representation of the maturation of Indian talent and served as a starting point for India's voyage in the world of international cricket.

Although the Parsi team's involvement was met with a variety of reactions by the English county sides they played against, this was an important step in demonstrating that Indian cricketers are capable of competing on an international level because of their participation. It effectively strengthened India's status in the global cricketing arena and created the groundwork for future cricket tours in India.

The Beginnings of Cricket in the United Kingdom:

Regional and domestic cricket events and competitions started to take shape as the popularity of cricket continued to rise among Indians. The Parsis, Hindus, Muslims, and Europeans all fielded teams in the tournament known as the Bombay Quadrangular, which is considered to be one of the earliest examples of a domestic competition played in India. This event did more than just provide local players a chance to show off their skills; it also stoked the fires of rivalry between players from surrounding areas.

In 1892, the All-India cricket team, which was headed by the Maharaja of Patiala, set out on a tour of England. During their time there, they left a profound impression on the cricketing establishment in England. This tour gave people even more reason to believe in India's cricketing potential and planted the seeds for India's participation in international cricket in the years to come.

The Board of Control for Cricket in India (BCCI) was established after the following events:

The establishment of the Board of Control for Cricket in India (BCCI) in December 1928 was a

watershed event in the progression of the sport of cricket in India. The Board of Control for Cricket in India (BCCI) was established as the governing authority for cricket in the country, with the duty of directing the growth, administration, and organization of the sport.

At Lord's Cricket Ground in 1932, India competed against England in its very first Test match, which was overseen by the Board of Control for Cricket in India (BCCI). It was a moment of enormous pride and significance for the nation of India as this occasion signified the official admission of India into international cricket.

The Period Following Independence:

When India gained its freedom in 1947, a new era began for the sport of cricket. The newly established nation's identity began to be reflected in and shaped by the sport not long after it was introduced. When India's cricket team competed on the international scene, it turned into a source of national pride and brought the country closer together.

Legendary cricket players like of Vinoo Mankad, Vijay Hazare, and Sunil Gavaskar began their rise to prominence in the 1950s and 1960s. They were able to boost the profile of Indian cricket and inspire faith in the talents of Indian cricket players as a result of their performances.

The Memorable Victory at the World Cup in 1983:

The 1983 Cricket World Cup is seen as one of the most important turning points in the long and illustrious history of Indian cricket. The Indian cricket team, captained by Kapil Dev, astonished the rest of the cricketing world by winning the championship match against the West Indies. The triumph was India's first ever at the World Cup, and it is sometimes regarded as a watershed moment in the country's climb to the top of the cricketing world.

The victory at the World Cup in 1983 not only cemented India's position as a major player on the international cricketing scene, but it also caught the nation's imagination. The victory of the underdog resonated with people from all different walks of life because it became a symbol of hope, determination, and the ability to achieve what appears to be impossible.

The Modern Era, Sachin Tendulkar, and Cricket:

The decades of the 1990s and the early 2000s were pivotal in Sachin Tendulkar's ascent to prominence; he would go on to become one of the most legendary personalities in the annals of cricket. Tendulkar became a cricketing legend as a result of his record-breaking

accomplishments and his ability to bring the entire country together via his exploits.

Indian cricket has been given a fresh lease on life ever since the inaugural season of the Indian Premier League (IPL) in 2008. The Indian Premier League has become a worldwide sensation, drawing the best players from all over the world and fundamentally altering how cricket is perceived and played in India.

Equality of women and men and inclusiveness:

The game of cricket has progressed to the point in India where women's cricket is now an

important and well-respected aspect of the sport. The dominance of the Indian women's cricket team, particularly in the most recent years, has helped to dis-prove traditional gender roles and contributed to the advancement of women's rights in their nation. Mithali Raj and Harmanpreet Kaur are two examples of successful female cricketers who have emerged as inspirational figures for younger players.

Dynamic Patterns of Caste and Inclusivity:

Cricket has also presented a challenge to the caste hierarchies that are strongly ingrained in Indian society. The activity has opened doors of opportunity for persons from underrepresented castes, allowing them to rise to prominence and overcome social preconceptions in the process. Players like Vinod Kambli and Pravin Amre, who come from less privileged families, are examples of the transforming impact of cricket in eradicating caste-based inequality.

Concerning Difficulties and Controversies:

The sport of cricket in India has seen its fair share of difficulties and controversy throughout the years. The sport's reputation was damaged by scandals involving match-fixing that occurred in the late 1990s and early 2000s. There have been instances where the game has been overshadowed by corruption, power battles within the administration of cricket, and ethical conundrums.

The Importance of This to Culture

The game of cricket is strongly rooted in the social and cultural traditions of India. Not only does it have a place on the field, but it also has a position in the world of literature, art, music, and film. The lingo and metaphors associated with cricket are smoothly integrated into ordinary discussion. In many Indian homes, the televisions are usually tuned to cricket broadcasts, thus the roar of the crowd can be heard in the background.

Cricket is more than just a sport; it's also a way to pass the time with friends, a fun way to meet new people, and a great way to strengthen relationships. Families, friends, and acquaintances get together to watch matches together, and they rejoice over victory and commiserate over losses as a group. The cricket stadium is a location where emotions run strong, and the passion of the crowd is contagious; examples include Kolkata's traditional Eden Gardens and Mumbai's modern Wankhede Stadium.

The Cricket World Cup, the Twenty20 World Cup, and the Indian Premier League have all evolved into massive cultural festivities that include music, dance, and pyrotechnics in addition to their traditional roles as international athletic competitions. The Indian diaspora might feel a stronger feeling of connection to their homeland through the sport of cricket, which is one reason why they consider it to be an essential component of their cultural identity.

The narrative of cricket's historical setting in India is one of evolution, transition, and cultural assimilation. Cricket is much more than just a sport; it has evolved into an essential component of Indian culture over the course of its history, from its origins in British colonial times and the early contributions of Parsi pioneers to the successes and setbacks of the modern period. It has broken down barriers and been a driving force behind social progress, empowerment, and cohesion all at the same time.

The game of cricket in India exemplifies the persistent capacity of sport to both reflect and influence the culture in which it thrives by seizing the hearts and imaginations of millions of people all over the country.

3. **Overview of the book's purpose and structure**

The article "Cricket as a Catalyst for Social Change in India" is a comprehensive investigation into the multidimensional function that cricket plays in creating the social dynamics of one of the world's most culturally diverse nations, India. The purpose of this book is to convey a profound knowledge of how, below its surface as a sport, cricket has become a catalyst for change, reflecting and influencing the vast tapestry of Indian society. This book tries to show the enormous impact that cricket has had on several parts of Indian life, including national identity, gender equality, caste dynamics, regional unity, education, and philanthropy. It does so by providing an in-depth examination of the topic, as well as a rich historical backdrop and fascinating narratives to illustrate the impact.

Function of the Book:

The primary purpose of the book is to shed light on the transformative ability of cricket as a vehicle for social change in India. [Cricket] is the national sport of India. The purpose of this project is to bring attention to the crucial part that sports have played in subverting social conventions, removing boundaries, and promoting inclusiveness. The purpose of this book is to demonstrate, via research into the historical, cultural, and modern aspects of cricket in India, the significant ways in which the game has had an impact on and contributed to the development of the social structure of the country.

The book also aims to address the issues and controversies that have afflicted Indian cricket. It does this by providing a balanced perspective on the ethical dilemmas and obstacles that the sport has encountered throughout its journey. Additionally, the book promises to provide insights into the future of cricket in India by studying emerging patterns and prospective areas for increased social impact. This will allow the book to present a road map for the sport's sustained role in promoting good change within Indian society.

The Organization of the Book:

The content of this book is organized into a number of thematic chapters, each of which examines a distinct facet of cricket's function as a driving force behind social transformation in India. It starts off with an in-depth introduction that lays the groundwork for the subsequent investigation of cricket's significance and influence. The introduction also provides a concise outline of the aim and structure of the book, giving out the roadmap for readers to follow as they navigate the various and complex storylines that are presented in the remaining chapters.

The following chapters examine cricket's impact on Indian culture from a variety of perspectives, each focusing on a specific facet of cricket's effect. Each chapter goes deeply into a distinct topic, providing a full overview of the subject at hand by delivering historical context, modern analysis, and entertaining tales about the issue at hand in each chapter. Each chapter gives a comprehensive analysis of the complex link that exists between cricket and Indian society. This relationship is examined from the historical foundations of cricket in India to the impact it has had on national identity, gender equality, and caste dynamics.

In addition, the book has specific chapters that investigate the impact that cricket has had on regional cohesion, educational opportunities, and social activities. These sections show the ways in which cricket has transformed educational expectations, provided as a forum for humanitarian activities and social responsibility, and developed a sense of community and pride among people from many locations.

In addition to this, the book discusses the difficulties and scandals that have played a role in the development of the story of Indian cricket. It provides readers with a complete grasp of the complexity and nuances that underlay cricket's journey in India by offering an in-depth examination of the ethical difficulties, match-fixing scandals, and administrative struggles that have questioned the integrity of the sport. In addition, it provides readers with an overview of the history of cricket in India.

The final section of the book offers a look into the foreseeable future of cricket in India. It does so by analyzing developing tendencies and speculating on possible areas for greater societal effect. It sheds light on the ways in which the sport can continue to be a force for good and contribute to the larger social and cultural environment of the nation.

Chapter 1

Cricket and National Identity

Cricket is more than just a sport; it is also a cultural phenomenon and an essential component of the national identities of a great number of countries. Cricket is more than just a sport for many nations, including India, Pakistan, Australia, England, and the West Indies; it is a source of national pride and a representation of the countries' distinct identities. This essay dives into the complex relationship that exists between cricket and national identity, examining the ways in which the sport has influenced and mirrored the history, culture, and geopolitical climate of a number of different countries.

The Development of Cricket Throughout History

Cricket can be traced all the way back to England in the 16th century, where it was first played as a country pastime in various cities and villages around the country. Over the course of several centuries, it developed into an organized sport that adheres to a set of predetermined rules and guidelines. Cricket was quickly adopted as a popular sport on every continent thanks in large part to the efforts of the British Empire, which helped spread the game throughout its many territories. As a direct consequence of this, cricket was an essential component in the formation of the national identities of many countries that were governed by the British.

The Colonial Legacy: Cricket, a Sport Introduced by the British

Cricket was brought to a number of countries by the British during their colonial rule, and as a result, the game came to represent the British way of life. The game was not just a form of recreation but also an instrument of cultural imperialism in many parts of the world. In places such as India and the West Indies, the sport of cricket came to be identified with the colonial power, and the ruling British elite utilized the sport as a means of demonstrating their cultural and racial superiority.

The early years of cricket in these colonies were marked by racial inequality, with indigenous groups being excluded from the game. [Cricket] was introduced to the Americas by British colonists. Cricket, on the other hand, became a center of resistance and the statement of national identity as the fight for independence gained steam. The beginning of this new phase in the relationship between cricket and national identity was characterized by the transformation of the sport from a symbol of British power into a symbol of resistance.

The Game of Cricket as a Method of Opposition

Cricket was an important part of the struggle for independence in a number of different countries. Indian cricket, for example, saw the rise of characters like as Lala Amarnath and C.K. Nayudu, who used the sport as a platform to challenge British colonialism and advance Indian nationalism. The All-India Cricket Team, which was captained by the affable Lala Amarnath and represented the hopes of a people that yearned for independence, was headed by the charismatic Amarnath.

Cricket became a unifying force and a source of pride for the descendants of African slaves who had been taken to the West Indies during the time of the trans-atlantic slave trade. Many of these descendants live in the West Indies. The popularity of cricket skyrocketed during this time, and players from the West Indies, like as Sir Garfield Sobers and Sir Frank Worrell, became icons of rebellion against the per-secution of the colonial government. The domination of the West Indies cricket team in the 1970s and 1980s not only helped to firmly establish their national identity but also had a significant influence on how the rest of the world views the Caribbean.

The Putting Together of National Teams

As nations achieved independence from one another, they started to organize their very own national cricket teams. When this happened, a considerable departure oc-curred from the previous practice of playing on regional teams, which were frequently separated along colonial lines. The establishment of national teams gave these nations the opportunity to represent themselves on the world stage and to highlight the unique aspects of their identities in the process.

In 1947, the division of India into two parts resulted in the birth of a new country, which came to be known as Pakistan. Cricket was a significant factor in the successful effort to unite a heterogeneous community behind a single banner. Players such as Hanif Mohammad and Fazal Mahmood were symbols of national unity, and Paki-stan's triumph over England in the Oval Test in 1954 is still regarded as a watershed event in the country's long and illustrious history of cricket.

In a similar manner, Australia utilized cricket as a method to develop a distinct national identity that was distinct from its colonial background. Since it began in 1882, the Ashes series played between Australia and England has become one of the most intense rivalries in all of cricket. It was regarded as a defining moment in Australian identity that Australia's victory in the Bicentennial Test in 1988, which commemorated 200 years of European settlement in Australia, brought about.

Cricket and the Construction of Cultural Identity

The Way in Which Cricket Has Influenced Both Language and Popular Culture

Cricket has had a significant impact on the cultural identities of nations, having an influence on not only language and literature but also music, popular culture, and even popular culture. Cricket has had a pervasive influence on the vernacular in nations like India and Pakistan, where its phrases and idioms have become commonplace. As an illustration, the expression "it's not cricket" is frequently utilized to refer to behavior that is unfair or unethical.

In addition, the sport of cricket has served as a wellspring of creativity for writers. Novels like "A Corner of a Foreign Field" by Ramachandra Guha and "Beyond a Boundary" by C.L.R. James investigates the complex connection between cricket and a country's sense of national identity. Not only do these books go into the history of the sport, but they also provide insights into the social features of the countries that are represented in the sport.

The Diaspora and the Role of Cricket in Defining Identity

The Indian and Pakistani diasporas have spread their love of cricket to many different countries and regions around the world. Cricket continues to be an important cultural marker for South Asian groups in nations such as the United Kingdom, Canada, and Australia. These countries have seen an increase in the number of cricket clubs, tournaments, and leagues, which have provided residents with a sense of belonging and a connection to their countries of origin.

The diaspora's celebration of holidays like Diwali and Eid often include cricket matches as an integral element of the festivities. This is one way in which cricket has contributed to the formation of the diaspora's cultural identity. The complex cultural fabric that cricket creates, linking people across countries and generations, is brought to mind by these events, which serve as a reminder of that rich cultural tapestry.

The Importance of Cricket's Greatest Players

Legends of the game of cricket have been instrumental in the formation of the national identities of the countries they represent. Iconic players on the cricket field, such as Sachin Tendulkar in India, Imran Khan in Pakistan, Brian Lara in the West Indies, and Sir Don Bradman in Australia, have gone beyond the confines of the sport to become national symbols in their respective countries.

Their impressive careers, magnetic personalities, and exemplary leadership have established them as cultural ambassadors for their respective nations.

They are not merely sportsmen; rather, they are living legends whose tales and exploits are told from one generation to the next, so reinforcing the relationship between cricket and a country's sense of national identity.

The Relationship Between Cricket and Sociopolitical Identity
Both diplomacy and geopolitics are involved.

Cricket has been utilized as an instrument of diplomacy and geopolitics, reflecting the intricate nature of the relationships that exist between countries. Cricket diplomacy has been utilized frequently by India and Pakistan, two nuclear-armed neighbors who have a history of confrontation, in order to de-escalate the situation. The political significance of games played between India and Pakistan, also known as "Indo-Pak" confrontations, cannot be overstated. They provide opportunity for people-to-people encounters, as well as opportunities for diplomacy and even initiatives to resolve conflicts.

The revival of cricketing links between India and Pakistan, in addition to those between India and other countries, may be an indication of the warming of bilateral relations. On the other hand, if cricketing links between two countries are severed, it may be a sign that relations are deteriorating between the two countries.

The Importance of Symbols of the Nation

The fact that cricket serves as a stage for the performance of national anthems and emblems helps to further establish the sport's connection to the concept of national identity. It is a moment for the nation to come together and feel a sense of pride when the flag of their country is raised or when a player dons the national shirt of their team. The playing of national anthems before to sporting events is known to evoke feelings of patriotism and to instill a stronger sense of belonging to a bigger community.

During the thrilling Cricket World Cup final in 2019, England prevailed against Australia in a super over, which served as a prime example of the emotional link that exists between cricket and national emblems. The combination of cricket, national symbols, and identity was exemplified by the scene in which the English team sang "God Save the Queen" while wrapped in the Union Jack.

Authenticity and Openness to All

In spite of the fact that cricket has played a crucial part in the process of national identity formation, the sport has struggled with issues relating to diversity and representation.

Historically, the sport was dominated by affluent white males, and communities of indigenous people and people of color were not allowed to participate. Cricket started to reflect these developments as nations got more diverse and more inclusive over the course of the game's history.

For instance, the West Indies cricket team initially consisted predominately of players of Afro-Caribbean descent, but in subsequent years it included players of Indian, Pakistani, and mixed ethnicity as well. This eclectic composition underlined the idea that unity may be found in variety, and it paralleled the growing identity of the Caribbean nations.

Players on the Australian national team began to come from a variety of cultural backgrounds, such as Usman Khawaja and Fawad Ahmed, who were both born in Pakistan. This trend continued in recent years. Their presence posed a challenge to the conventional understanding of Australian identity and exemplified the multiculturalism that has come to characterize the nation in modern times.

Within the Context of a Globalized Sport

Cricket has emerged as a really international sport thanks to the globalization that has occurred in the world in recent decades. This process of internationalization has been sped up by the development of Twenty20 cricket and leagues such as the Indian Premier League (IPL). Players from a variety of countries now compete in leagues located in other countries, resulting in the creation of a cricketing community that is both diverse and interconnected.

The relationship between cricket and national identity is affected in both a positive and a bad way by the globalization that has taken place. On the one hand, it encourages the exchange of different cultures and brings people all over the world together. On the other side, there are many who maintain that it watered out the singularity of the national identity by fostering a more standardized culture of cricket.

Cricket and a country's sense of national identity are inextricably linked, and the nature of that connection is dynamic and ever-shifting. The enormous impact that the sport has had on a nation's identity can be seen in the historical legacy of colonialism, the use of cricket as an instrument of resistance, the establishment of national teams, and the influence on culture, language, and geopolitics.

In spite of cricket's ongoing development in an increasingly globalized world, the sport continues to serve as a symbol of togetherness, pride, and national consciousness.

It serves as a potent reminder of the pervasive impact that history, culture, and politics have had and continue to have on the sporting arena. Cricket is more than just a game; it is a mirror that reflects the complex and unique characteristics of countries all over the world.

1.1 The role of cricket in shaping India's national identity

In India, cricket is more than simply a sport; it is also a cultural phenomenon, a national passion, and a reflection of the identity of the country. Over the course of more than a century, cricket has been an essential component in the formation and reflection of India's national identity. This essay investigates the significant influence that cricket has had on the formation of India's national identity by analyzing the sport's historical background, cultural relevance, and sociopolitical implications.

Contextualization of the Past

The British colonialists are credited with introducing cricket to India in the 18th century, which is when the sport's origins in India can be traced back to. In the beginning, the British people that had moved abroad played cricket as a form of pleasure for themselves and their children. Due to the fact that it was considered a sport for gentlemen, the British used it as a tool to assert their dominance over the native Indian people.

Cricket, on the other hand, went through a period of transition about the same time that India's fight for independence gained steam. It evolved into a forum in which people could voice their opposition to British colonial control. It was recognized by prominent Indian leaders such as Mahatma Gandhi and Jawaharlal Nehru that the sport had the ability to build a feeling of national identity while also helping to mobilize large groups of people.

The Role of Cricket as a Means of Promoting Nationalism

Lala Amarnath and C.K. Nayudu Were Two of the Early Pioneers

The decade of the 1930s was an important one in the annals of India's cricket history. Not only did they flourish on the field, but they also utilized cricket as a means to advocate the cause of Indian nationalism throughout this decade. Figures like Lala Amarnath and C.K. Nayudu emerged as cricketing pioneers during this decade. They did this by using cricket as a medium to champion the cause of Indian nationalism.

During the time when India was fighting for its independence from the British, the charismatic all-rounder Lala Amarnath became a symbol of defiance against the British. Because of his courageous play on the cricket field and his outspoken personality, he became a hero to millions of Indians and an inspiration to others.

The work done by Amarnath cleared the path for subsequent generations of Indian players to represent their country with honor and dignity on the cricket field.

The Test Series of 1947: A Crucial Turning Point

The Test series that took place in 1947 between India and England was a momentous occasion for the country. It was the first Test series that India played as an independent nation, and it marked the beginning of a new era. India won all three matches in the series. It was a credit to the Indian team's resolve and resiliency that they were able to come out on top in the fifth and final Test of the series, which took place at The Oval. This triumph not only established India's presence on the international cricketing arena, but it also strengthened the connection between the sport and India's sense of national identity.

The Long and Winding Road to World Cup Victory

The Cricket World Cup that India competed in and won in 1983 has a significant impact on the country's cricketing legacy. An inexperienced but resolute Indian squad, captained by Kapil Dev, surprised and stunned the West Indies to win the tournament's championship game and write themselves into the annals of cricket history. A nation that has long desired for respect in the world of cricket experienced a moment of elation and pride after achieving that recognition thanks to this success.

It was not only about cricket when India won the World Cup in 1983; rather, it was a symbol of the nation's ability to prevail over adversity and it inspired a sense of national solidarity and patriotism. It encouraged people to believe that India could achieve success on the international stage in any area of endeavor.

Importance in terms of Culture

Expressions of Language and Their Use

The game of cricket has had a huge impact on the culture and language of India. The lingo and idioms used in cricket have effortlessly merged into regular conversation. In India, phrases such as "batsman," "duck," "hat-trick," and "sixer" are frequently used to describe a variety of events, and not simply in the context of cricket; these phrases are employed in everyday life as well.

The distinctive cricketing nicknames that have been conferred upon cherished players are another indication of the sport's cultural effect. Icons such as Sachin

Tendulkar, also known as the "Little Master" or "Master Blaster," Virender Sehwag, also known as the "Nawab of Najafgarh," and Rahul Dravid, affectionately referred to as "The Wall," have become names that are familiar to most people and have become cultural symbols.

Bollywood's Take on Cricket

Cricket and Bollywood, two of India's most beloved cultural institutions, have frequently collaborated to produce defining moments in the history of Indian society. The sport of cricket has served as the setting for a number of films produced in Bollywood, which tell stories revolving around passion, rivalry, and victory. Films such as "Lagaan," "Iqbal," and "Dil Bole Hadippa!" have all paid tribute to the significant role that cricket has played in shaping the cultural landscape of India.

In addition, cricket has spawned a new subgenre of films known as sports dramas. These films represent the challenges and victories faced by aspiring cricket players. These films have inspired the ambitions of numerous young people all over the country.

The Power of Cricket to Bring People Together

Cricket possesses a special power that enables it to bring together a country as complex and varied as India. Cricket has the capacity to unite individuals from all walks of life, regardless of factors such as caste, religion, language, or social background. The roar of the audience, the playing of the national anthem before a match, and the excitement of a cricketing competition all contribute to the creation of a sense of shared identity.

Since its inception in 2008, the Indian Premier League (IPL) has been instrumental in bringing people together from all over the country's many regions and states. As a result of the franchise system used in the IPL, players from all over India are able to compete for different towns, which helps to cultivate a pan-Indian sense of identity.

Dimensions of Socio Political Life

Cricket as a Medium of Diplomacy

Cricket has had a one-of-a-kind impact on India's diplomatic efforts and its relationships with other countries. The animosity with archrival Pakistan has frequently been defused and bridges have been built through the use of cricket matches as a diplomatic weapon. Cricket has created opportunities for individuals from both countries to communicate with one another and share their cultures, despite the difficulty that has been present in the political relationship between the two nations.

The Impact of Some of Cricket's Greatest Players

Not only have legendary Indian cricket players such as Sachin Tendulkar, Kapil Dev, and Sunil Gavaskar been successful on the field of play, but they have also transcended the realm of sport to become revered figures in Indian culture.

These cricket players exemplify the virtues of endurance, humility, and dedication, representing the hopes and dreams of millions of people living in India.

In particular, Tendulkar, who became known as the "God of Cricket," became a symbol of India's tenacity and fervor during this time. Through the course of his record-breaking career, which spanned over twenty years, he became a revered figure who brought the country together, transcending both regional and linguistic barriers.

The Commercial Side of Cricket

The process of making cricket a commercial sport has had a profound effect on India's sense of national identity. The Board of Control for Cricket in India (BCCI), which oversees cricket in India, is one of the most financially stable cricket governing bodies in the world. The large viewership and sponsorship deals associated with Indian cricket have not only helped to the expansion of the sport, but they have also fueled India's economy and propelled the nation to a prominent position on the global stage.

The Indian Premier League in particular has grown into a worldwide sensation, drawing in players, broadcasters, and sponsors from all over the world. It has ushered in a new era of dominance for Indian cricket and raised the country's profile in the international cricketing community.

It cannot be denied that cricket has played a significant part in the formation of India's national identity. Cricket has been an indispensable component of India's development as a nation at every stage, from its beginnings as a resistance movement against British colonialism to its current status as a unifying force with profound cultural importance. The sport has moved beyond the confines of only being a game, becoming instead a mirror that reflects the variety, passion, and pride of a nation with more than a billion people in it.

Cricket has not only brought forth triumphs and moments of happiness, but it has also served as a wellspring of motivation, aspiration, and solidarity. Cricket is a living witness to India's ability to overcome obstacles, appreciate diversity, and present its own personality to the rest of the globe as the country continues its process of modernization. It is more than just a sport; it is an expression of the very spirit and essence of India.

1.2 Iconic moments in Indian cricket history

The annals of Indian cricket are replete with legendary games and matches that have etched themselves permanently into the collective consciousness of the country. These moments not only signify victories on the cricket field, but they also represent the ambitions, desires, and aspirations of millions of cricket fans in India. India is home to some of the most passionate cricket fans in the world. In this essay, we dig into some of the most famous moments in the history of Indian cricket, chronicling the path of the sport in the country from its earliest days up till the present day.

The Year 1952 Marks India's First Test Win

India's first-ever victory in a Test match, which took place against England at Madras (now known as Chennai) in 1952, is considered to be one of the most important moments in Indian cricket history. An historic victory was won by the Indian squad, which was captained by Vijay Hazare. This event served as a turning point for Indian cricket, as it was at this time that the

country at long last declared itself to be a formidable opponent on the world stage.

Against the backdrop of post-independence euphoria, the win was more than just a sporting achievement; it reflected India's emergence as a cricketing nation, hungry to compete and shine in the world of cricket. In other words, the win marked India's emergence as a nation that is eager to excel in the world of cricket.

During the 1983 Cricket World Cup, Kapil Dev scored 175 not out

An unforgettable event took place at the 1983 Cricket World Cup, which was hosted in England. This event irrevocably altered Indian cricket. After losing early wickets in the championship match against the formidable West Indies, India found themselves in a perilous position. When Indian team captain Kapil Dev stepped to the crease, his side's score was 17 for 5, and they were reeling. What ensued was undoubtedly one of the most legendary innings in the history of cricket.

After facing 138 balls, Kapil Dev hit an undefeated 175 runs, bringing India's score up to 266 and rescuing them from a potentially disastrous position. This innings not only led to India's first triumph in the Cricket World Cup, but it also sparked a revolution in the sport of cricket across the nation. The excitement and drive displayed by Kapil Dev won the hearts of the nation and served as an inspiration to a whole new generation of cricket players.

Desert Storm, Sachin Tendulkar's Performance in 1998

Throughout his career, Sachin Tendulkar, who is frequently referred to as the "God of Cricket," was responsible for a great number of famous moments. One of the most noteworthy ones occurred in Sharjah in 1998, when the Coca-Cola Cup was held there.

During a rain-interrupted encounter against Australia, India was in danger of being eliminated from the competition and needed to score 276 runs in 46 overs in order to advance to the finals.

The innings that Tendulkar played was nothing less than spectacular. He single-handedly led India to victory with a record-setting performance, scoring 143 runs while suffering from cramping and playing in scorching heat. Fans of cricket will never forget the moment when Tendulkar reached his century and looked up to the heavens in celebration. It was illustrative of his devotion, determination, and knowledge of the game in question.

The Test Match at Eden Gardens in 2001 Between India and Australia

Many people consider the second Test match of the 2001 series between India and Australia at Eden Gardens in Kolkata to be one of the most dramatic turnarounds in the history of Test cricket. This match was part of a series between India and Australia. After being bowled out for just 171 runs in the first innings, India was already behind in the series and faced the prospect of having to face a follow-on. It appeared like victory would come easily for Australia.

What occurred next, on the other hand, was nothing short of a miracle. Laxman's score of 281 and Dravid's contribution of 180 contributed to a remarkable partnership that was built by VVS Laxman and Rahul Dravid. India scored 657 runs, giving Australia a score of 384 to beat their aim. The match was won by India by a score of 171 runs thanks to the outstanding bowling performance of Harbhajan Singh, which included a hat-trick. This epic comeback triumph exemplified the never-give-up mentality of Indian cricket players and coaches alike.

The Match-Winning Six Hit by MS Dhoni in the Cricket World Cup Final in 2011

The sequence that ended with MS Dhoni hitting a magnificent six over long-on will be remembered for all time as the defining moment of the 2011 ICC Cricket World Cup final. Dhoni, the captain of the Indian squad, walked up to the crease as the team was under duress and chasing the mark set by Sri Lanka. He not only guided India to victory with an undefeated 91 but also clinched the victory with a gigantic six. His performance was pivotal in India's success.

Millions of people in India cheered enthusiastically as the ball was launched into the night sky over Mumbai. This victory was especially noteworthy because it occurred on home territory, and the picture of Dhoni maintaining his composure and cool manner in the face of intense pressure exemplified the attributes of captaincy and leadership that he possesses.

The Border-Gavaskar Trophy was Won by India in the 2018-2019 Season

The Border-Gavaskar Trophy series that took place in Australia in 2018-19 is a demonstration of India's resiliency and commitment in the face of adverse conditions.

In spite of the fact that they dropped the first test in Adelaide, India were able to come back and win the series by a score of 2-1, which was their first victory in a Test series played in Australia.

Cheteshwar Pujara's colossal batting effort, Jasprit Bumrah's great bowling, and India's historic victory in Melbourne are three of the standout events from this series. Other noteworthy moments include Jasprit Bumrah's outstanding bowling. These events not only demonstrated India's newly discovered power in overseas Tests but also solidified the team's status as a formidable force in international cricket. India is now widely regarded as one of the top teams in the world.

The Century Scored on One Leg by Virat Kohli in 2019

Virat Kohli, the captain of the Indian cricket team, created a legendary moment of grit and drive during a test match played against England at Trent Bridge in 2018. Even though he had hurt his back in the previous game, Kohli insisted on playing through the pain. He batted through the agony and ended up scoring 97 runs in the first inning of the game. In spite of this, the event that came to symbolize his entire career was when he scored a century in the second innings while batting on only one leg.

The fact that Kohli scored 103 runs without losing a game demonstrates his unwavering dedication to both his team and country. This demonstrated that he is not only one of the best batsmen in the world, but also a leader who is willing to do whatever in his power to ensure the success of his team.

Historic victory for India in the Test Series played in Australia in 2020-21

The Border-Gavaskar Trophy competition that will take place in Australia in 2020-21 will go down as one of the most memorable events in the annals of Indian cricket. In addition to having some key players out due to injury or other commitments, India was up against a tough Australian side. In spite of the challenges it faced, India was able to emerge triumphant and win the series 2-1.

Ajinkya Rahane's century in Melbourne and the outstanding performances of young players like Shardul Thakur and Washington Sundar were two key moments that represented India's grit and tenacity throughout the series. India's standing as a dominant power in international cricket was reaffirmed thanks to the team's victory in the series, which also marked a landmark occasion in the history of the squad.

The history of Indian cricket is replete with famous events that represent the nation's passion for the sport, its tenacity in the face of hardship, and its persistent determination to excel on the international arena.

These events transcend the confines of the cricket pitch; they become ingrained in India's cultural fabric, acting as sources of inspiration for succeeding generations and as emblems of national pride.

These classic moments depict the path of Indian cricket, from the early days of Test cricket to the modern era of T20 extravaganzas. They emphasize the achievements of renowned cricketers and the spirit of working together as a team. They are a tribute to the everlasting love affair that has existed between India and the sport of cricket, an affair that continues to develop and flourish, producing new legendary moments on a daily basis.

1.3 Influence of cricket on cultural, social, and political developments

Cricket is more than simply a sport; it is a phenomenon that has left an everlasting effect on the culture, society, and politics of the nations who love it. Cricket has had a significant impact on a variety of cultural, social, and political movements ever since it was first played in England in the 16th century and has since grown to become a popular sport played all over the world. Within the scope of this article, we will investigate how the sport of cricket has influenced and been influenced by these characteristics of the civilizations and nations located all over the world.

The influence of culture

Expressions of Language and Their Use

In the countries in which it is played, cricket has had a substantial impact on the vocabulary and idioms that are used. Many phrases and idioms that originate from cricket have made their way into ordinary speech and are now used to describe a wide range of activities and scenarios that have nothing to do with the sport. The term "it's not cricket" is used to refer to unjust behavior, while the term "batsman" is used to refer to a person who is in a difficult situation. Additionally, the phrase "getting caught behind" is used to refer to someone who is exposed. These expressions have made their way into common language.

These statements are a reflection of cricket's profound incorporation into the cultural fabric of nations and the sport's pervasive presence in everyday life. They are a living monument to the sport's ever-present impact on the communication and lexicon of the people.

The Fine Arts and Written Word

Numerous novels, poetry, and paintings have been created in tribute to the sport of cricket, making it an influential source of creativity in the arts. These pieces investigate the subtleties of the game, as well as its cultural relevance and the feelings that it elicits in both the players and the spectators.

C.L.R. James's "Beyond a Boundary" and Ramachandra Guha's "A Corner of a Foreign Field" are two examples of books that delve into the cultural and historical aspects of cricket in the West Indies and India, respectively. These studies offer new perspectives on the enormous influence that sport has had on the culture and society of the countries in question.

Performing Arts and Musical Expression

Additionally, cricket has made its way into the fields of music and entertainment. Songs and movies with a cricket theme are particularly well received in nations where the citizens have a strong emotional attachment to the sport of cricket.

The calypso song "Cricket, Lovely Cricket" was written and performed in the West Indies to honor the cultural relevance of the sport of cricket. Bollywood, the prolific film industry of India, has created a number of movies with cricket as the central theme. One of these is titled "Lagaan," which uses the narrative of a cricket match as a metaphor for the struggle against British colonial control. Bollywood has produced a number of movies with cricket as the central theme.

The impact of society

In Harmony with Our Differences

Cricket has the extraordinary power to bring together people from very different backgrounds. Cricket is a sport that overcomes linguistic, religious, and geographical barriers in countries such as India, Pakistan, and the West Indies. It is a unifying force that brings people together. When the national cricket team competes, millions of fans from all walks of life and eras come together to show their support for their country.

The Indian Premier League (IPL) is a wonderful illustration of the harmony that can be found within diversity. The Indian Premier League brings together players from all around the world to participate on teams that represent their respective cities. This multifaceted composition exemplifies the multicultural and multiethnic makeup of India and contributes to the development of a sense of national unity.

Both diplomacy and geopolitics are involved

Cricket has frequently been utilized as a diplomatic and geopolitical tool during the course of its history. The political tensions between two nations that are rivals can either be alleviated or increased by a match between them.

The Indo-Pak cricket series is the most renowned example of cricket diplomacy, since it has been used as a tool to establish discussion and reduce enmity between the two countries. Cricket matches have been played between India and Pakistan.

Cricket, on the other hand, has the potential to inflame political tensions. For example, cricket matches between India and Pakistan are not only fierce competitions on the field but also significant geopolitical events that capture the attention of people all over the world.

Heroes and Exemplars to Follow

The sport of cricket has produced a number of legendary players who have gone on to become the heroes and role models for innumerable fans. The accomplishments of these cricketers, together with their admirable personalities, serve as a source of motivation not just for aspiring cricket players but also for members of society as a whole.

Sachin Tendulkar is held in the highest regard throughout India and the rest of the world. He is known affectionately as the "Little Master" and is regarded as one of the best batsmen of all time. He is more than just a prominent figure in the world of sports; rather, he is emblematic of quality, humility, and dedication, and he serves as an example for individuals of all ages.

Political Sway as a Keyword

Movements for National Identities and Individual Freedoms

Cricket was an important part of the movement for independence for many countries that were formerly ruled by the British colonial government. Cricket was a tool that several nations, like India and the West Indies, utilized to affirm their national identities and fight back against British colonialism.

In India, cricket was used as a vehicle for expressing defiance and nationalism throughout turbulent times. The names Lala Amarnath and C.K. Nayudu are often cited as examples of early cricketing champions who personified the aspirations of the Indian people for freedom. Amarnath was the captain of the All-India Cricket Team, which embodied the aspirations of a nation fighting for its independence.

Cricket has been a unifying force and a source of pride for people in the West Indies who are descended from African slaves. Personages like as Sir Garfield Sobers and Sir Frank Worrell exemplified defiance in the face of tyranny by colonial authorities.

The domination of the West Indies cricket team in the 1970s and 1980s not only helped to firmly establish their national identity but also had a significant influence on how the rest of the world views the Caribbean.

Identities of Nations and Their Symbols

The fact that cricket serves as a stage for the performance of national anthems and emblems helps to further establish the sport's connection to the concept of national identity. The moment a player dons the national jersey or the flag of the country is raised is a moment for the nation to feel pride and unity in a shared experience.

Before cricket matches, national anthems are performed, and the sight of the national flag waving in the wind inspires a powerful sense of belonging as well as patriotism. These emblems are an important part of cricket matches since they serve as a reminder of the identity and history of the country.

Diplomacy with a Cricket Bat

There is a well-documented phenomena known as "cricketing diplomacy," in which countries use cricket matches to improve diplomatic relations with one another. The revival of cricketing connections between two countries, such as India and Pakistan or India and South Africa, for example, can be indicative of an improvement in the quality of relations between the two countries.

On the other hand, if cricketing links between two nations are severed, it may be an indication that relations are deteriorating. As a result, in addition to being a sport, cricket can also serve as a medium for diplomatic communication between countries.

Considerations Regarding the Economy and Business

The commercialization of cricket has resulted in substantial repercussions for both the economy and the political system. The sport brings in a significant amount of money thanks to the arrangements it does with sponsors, the television rights it acquires, and the products it sells. Due to the significant financial clout generated by the sport of cricket, cricket governing bodies such as the Board of Control for Cricket in India (BCCI) and Cricket Australia hold a significant amount of authority and influence.

Tournaments such as the Indian Premier League (IPL) have spawned enormous economic prospects, which in turn have attracted investments and attention from a wide variety of sectors. The political environment is impacted as a result of these financial effects due to the fact that cricket boards and administrators have a significant amount of control and influence in each of their various countries.

The game of cricket has had a significant and far-reaching impact on the cultural, social, and political evolution of the world. The game has made an everlasting imprint on the cultures of the countries and communities in which it is played. Its influence can be felt well beyond the perimeter ropes, permeating such realms as language, literature, music, and art. Cricket has the unique potential to bring together people of different backgrounds, so contributing to the development of a feeling of national identity and unity.

Cricket has been utilized as a diplomatic instrument in order to de-escalate tense situations and kickstart conversations between different nations. It has spawned famous characters who act as role models and heroes, motivating people not only interested in cricket but society as a whole. The commercialization of the sport has resulted in substantial economic and political repercussions, which in turn have shaped the administration and governance environment of cricket.

In a nutshell, cricket is more than simply a sport; it is a force that continues to evolve and influence the world in profound ways. This force is cultural, social, and political in nature. It is a genuinely extraordinary occurrence because of its ongoing history and the impact it has had on civilizations and nations.

Chapter 2

Breaking Barriers: Cricket and Gender Equality

Cricket, which is often regarded as a male-dominated activity, has a long history of being associated with concepts of masculinity and conventional gender norms. The landscape of cricket, on the other hand, has experienced substantial transformations over the course of the past few years as a result of deliberate attempts to advance gender equality and inclusivity within the sport. This essay examines the road that cricket has taken toward gender equality, examining the historical context, the problems that have been faced, and the strides that have been achieved in breaking down barriers and encouraging a more inclusive and equitable environment. Specifically, this essay focuses on the journey that cricket has taken toward the inclusion of women in the sport.

Disparities between Men's and Women's Cricket Teams in the Past

The history of cricket is littered with examples of discrimination against women, as this activity has always been off-limits to female participants. Cricket has always been considered as a male-dominated sport, and there were few options for female players to compete in organized tournaments or obtain professional instruction. The social mores and biases of the time frequently prevented women from actively participating in sports like cricket, relegating them instead to the spectator stands or to more casual, non-competitive situations.

The introduction of women's cricket in the latter half of the 19th century and the early part of the 20th century was a major step in the right direction. The dominance of men's cricket, on the other hand, continued to push it to the periphery and cast a shadow over it. The growth and development of women's cricket was hampered by a number of obstacles, including a lack of resources, inadequate finance, and a lack of infrastructure and support. These obstacles all worked together to make the sport more difficult to play.

The Obstacles That Women Must Overcome in Cricket

Obstacles of a Sociocultural Nature

There have been a number of important impediments to women's participation in cricket, including sociocultural conventions and preconceptions.

Current gender conventions frequently confined women to roles within the home, which discouraged their participation in sports, particularly those sports that were dominated by men, such as cricket. The idea that women cannot play cricket because of preconceived notions about their level of physical prowess and the perception that they are not interested in engaging in sports that involve competition has a long history.

Insufficient availability of resources and infrastructure

A significant obstacle has been presented by the fact that women's cricket does not have its own specialized infrastructure, training facilities, or resources. It was sometimes difficult for women's teams to locate adequate training fields, equipment, and coaching staff, which hampered their ability to improve their talents and compete at the top level. These difficulties have been worsened by the lack of money and sponsorship available for women's cricket, which has a chilling effect on the expansion and visibility of the sport.

Disparity in terms of opportunities and experiences

When compared to men's cricket, women's cricket has traditionally gotten much less coverage in the media and interest from the general public. Female cricket players have fewer opportunity to display their talent and be recognized for their accomplishments as a result of limited visibility and exposure, which led to these challenges. This lack of exposure not only had a negative effect on the popularity of the sport, but it also prevented the creation of role models and inspirational individuals for female cricket players who aspired to play the game.

Efforts Made Towards Achieving Gender Parity in the Sport of Cricket
Changes to both the Organization and its Policies

Cricket's governing boards and boards of control have been proactive in their efforts to eliminate gender imbalances and promote diversity in the sport. The introduction of dedicated women's cricket divisions, the adoption of gender equality policies, and the allocation of resources for the growth of women's cricket have all contributed considerably to the creation of an environment that is more suitable to the participation of female cricketers.

Through its Women's Cricket Strategy and a variety of other development projects, the International Cricket Council (ICC) has been a driving force in the movement to promote gender equality in the sport of cricket. At both the amateur and professional levels of the sport, these programs intend to offer women with equal access to opportunities, resources, and support for playing cricket.

Programs for Grassroots Development and Community Outreach

In the sport of cricket, grassroots development programs have been extremely helpful in both the cultivation of new talent and the cultivation of a culture of inclusivity. Young girls now have access to high-quality coaching and training thanks to programs like school outreach programs, coaching clinics, and talent identification camps, which have laid the groundwork for their participation in organized cricket. These camps also help identify young players with potential.

Not only have these grassroots programs helped encourage more females to take up cricket, but they have also contributed to addressing the social preconceptions and perceptions that society has toward women who participate in sports. These efforts have enabled girls to pursue their passion for cricket without the worry of being discriminated against or prejudiced against in any way. They do this by providing an environment that is supportive and encouraging.

Assistance with the Organization of Women's Cricket Leagues and Competitions

The development of women-specific cricket leagues and tournaments has been a significant step toward achieving gender parity in the sport. This has been a game-changing development. Female cricketers now have the opportunity to display their talents and compete at a professional level thanks to the establishment of leagues such as the Women's Big Bash League in Australia, the Women's Cricket Super League in England, and the Women's T20 Challenge in India.

Not only do these leagues provide opportunities for competitive play, but they also contribute to increasing the visibility of women's cricket and drawing in a wider audience. Changes in cultural perceptions and preconceptions have occurred as a result of increased media coverage and sponsorship of women's cricket leagues. These changes have brought greater attention to the athleticism and talent of female cricket players.

Campaigns for Advocacy and Raising Awareness

The advancement of gender equality and the elimination of discriminatory practices have been significantly aided by advocacy efforts and awareness campaigns in the sport of cricket. A greater awareness has been developed about the significance of gender inclusion in the sport of cricket as a result of campaigns that have highlighted the accomplishments of female cricket players, advocated for equal pay and opportunity, and focused on overcoming stereotypes.

A number of well-known cricketers, sports figures, and campaigners have added their voices to these initiatives in order to promote the cause of providing equal recognition and support for women's cricket. Their efforts have assisted in modifying public opinions and in creating an environment that is more welcoming and supportive for female cricket players.

The Effects That Gender Equality Has Had On Cricket
Participatory Democracy and Political Representation

Female cricketers now have the opportunity to pursue their passion and objectives without fear of experiencing discrimination or prejudice thanks to efforts to advance gender equality in the sport of cricket. Women have been able to achieve greater success in the sport as a result of increased access to opportunities, resources, and support, and they now act as role models and sources of inspiration for younger athletes. Not only has the participation of women in cricket helped to disprove common prejudices, but it has also made a contribution to the general movement toward the emancipation of women in society.

Alterations in Sociocultural Norms

The movement for gender equality in cricket has inspired broader social developments, which have posed a challenge to old gender conventions and stereotypes. The greater prominence and attention given to female cricket players has brought to light the significance of diversity and inclusivity in the sporting world. This change has had a domino effect, encouraging more girls and women to join in sports and achieve their athletic dreams. As a result, society as a whole has become more egalitarian and inclusive.

Development on Both the Economic and Social Fronts

The advancement of gender equality in cricket has not only helped to the sport's growth but also to economic and social progress. The expansion of infrastructure, the creation of employment opportunities, and the rise of auxiliary industries that are related with the sport of women's cricket have all resulted from increased investments and support for the women's version of the sport. This has, as a result, helped to contribute to the socioeconomic empowerment of women as well as the general development of communities.

In addition, the achievements and successes of female cricketers have assisted in challenging commonly held preconceptions regarding the skills and potential of females, so opening the way for a workforce that is more inclusive of and diverse in a number of different fields.

Challenges, as well as Prospects for the Future

In spite of the substantial headway that has been made, there are still many obstacles to overcome in the fight for gender equality in cricket. The gender pay gap, sexist attitudes in society, and inadequate coverage of women's cricket in the media all continue to act as roadblocks to the sport's expansion and progression. In order to address these issues, several stakeholders, such as cricket boards, policymakers, sponsors, and the media, would need to make ongoing efforts to develop a cricketing environment that is more egalitarian and welcoming to female cricket players.

A look to the future reveals that, in order to realize the full potential of gender equality in cricket, it will be essential to cultivate an inclusive culture, provide equal opportunities and resources, and advocate for equal representation and recognition. Not only will enabling the next generation of female cricketers and paving the road for their success completely alter the landscape of the sport, but it will also make a significant contribution to the development of a society that is more egalitarian and just. It is imperative that cricket players and advocates continue to fight for gender equality in order to ensure that cricket evolves into a sport that is open to all players, irrespective of gender.

The progress that cricket has made toward gender equality is illustrative of the transformative power of sport in terms of its ability to challenge societal norms and advance inclusiveness. Cricket has broken down barriers and established opportunities for women to participate, compete, and succeed in the sport from its beginnings as a male-dominated sport to its current status as a platform for female athletes to excel. Throughout its history, cricket has been dominated by men.

The advocacy and awareness efforts, the measures done by cricket boards, and the dedication of female cricketers have paved the road for a more inclusive and equitable future in cricket. The benefit of ensuring gender equality in cricket goes beyond the field of play, having an effect on broader sociocultural shifts and making a contribution to the growth of the economy and society.

It is important to note that despite cricket's ongoing development, the sport's dedication to gender equality has remained a driving force. This demonstrates cricket's capacity to motivate change and remove obstacles. Cricket is more than just a sport; rather, it is a metaphor for emancipation, representation, and the quest for a world that is more egalitarian and inclusive.

2.1 Evolution of women's cricket in India

Over the course of the last several decades in India, cricket, a sport that was traditionally seen as the preserve of men, has seen a remarkable transition, particularly with regard to the participation of women in cricket. In India, women's cricket has emerged from the shadow of its male counterpart to become a sport that is respected and extensively followed. This essay will delve into the evolution of women's cricket in India, tracing the key milestones, players, and challenges, as well as the significant impact it has had on the larger landscape of women's sports in the country. The journey of women's cricket in India is a story of determination, perseverance, and remarkable achievements.

Beginnings in Their Infancy:

In the early part of the 20th century, school and college teams in India played irregular matches of women's cricket, marking the sport's relatively humble beginnings in the country. However, it wasn't until the 1970s that women's cricket received the official status and structure it deserves. In 1973, a pivotal juncture in the development of women's cricket in India was marked by the establishment of the Women's Cricket Association of India (WCAI), which is considered to be a watershed moment in the sport's annals. Because to this establishment, female cricket players now have access to established competitions, selections, and opportunities.

The Coming of Age of Key Players

Diana Edulji was a trailblazing all-rounder who first appeared on the cricket scene in India in the early 1970s. She is considered to be one of the pioneers of women's cricket in India. She was a member of the India cricket team that competed in international matches and was a driving force behind the development of women's cricket as a competitive sport. Shanta Rangaswamy, Shubhangi Kulkarni, and Sandhya Agarwal were three more renowned performers during that era.

The decades of the 1970s and 1980s were crucial in establishing women's cricket as a competitive sport in India. These were the years when women's cricket was still in its infancy and players were vying for prominence as the sport became increasingly popular. This event marked the beginning of India's adventure in international women's cricket. The team went on its first international trip in 1976, when they visited the West Indies.

The Decade of the Nineties and the Emergence of Superstars:

The decade of the 1990s ushered in a fresh influx of passion and ability into the game of women's cricket in India. In the history of Indian women's cricket, notable figures include Anjum Chopra, Jhulan Goswami, and Mithali Raj, among others. In particular, Mithali Raj has established herself as a towering figure in the sport, elevating her status to that of an all-time great. Her accomplishments, level of commitment, and ability to lead have garnered her enormous respect not only in India but also across the globe.

Jhulan Goswami, who played the position of speed bowler, was another pioneer for Indian women's cricket. She went on to become the player with the most wickets taken in the history of women's One-Day Internationals (ODIs) and was an inspiration to a whole new generation of fast bowlers in India.

Achievements & Important Milestones:

During this time period, the Indian women's cricket team was able to accomplish a number of key goals and milestones.

In 2005, they competed in the Women's World Cup and made it all the way to the championship game, however they were ultimately unsuccessful. Nevertheless, because to this performance, women's cricket is now more widely known, and it has sparked the interest of fans all over the country.

The year 2017 marked India's second consecutive appearance in the ICC Women's World Cup final. This time, they were greeted by a fan base that was fervent and energetic, and it closely followed their voyage. The conclusion of the tournament at Lord's, which was witnessed by millions of cricket fans in India, was a watershed point in the progression of women's cricket in India. The enthusiastic play of India in the competition, led by Mithali Raj (who also served as team captain), contributed to the growing popularity of the sport.

What the Indian Premier League (IPL) Brings to the Table:

It's safe to say that the Indian Premier League (IPL) is largely responsible for the meteoric rise in popularity of cricket across India, and that includes women's cricket as well. As part of the festivities surrounding the Indian Premier League (IPL), there was a competition called the Women's T20 Challenge. This competition gave female cricket players the opportunity to compete alongside their male counterparts and show off their skills. The Women's T20 Challenge has garnered more attention as a result of the growing number of foreign players who take part in it and the expanding number of people that watch it.

Alterations to the Form of the Family Home:

Improvements have also been made to the domestic structure of women's cricket in India. These changes have been important. The Women's T20 league matches, Women's Senior One Day Trophy, and Women's T20 Challenger Trophy were all introduced to provide growing talent with competitive opportunities and exposure to the sport. Because of the increased emphasis placed on grassroots development and age-group contests, the national squad has been receiving a consistent stream of youthful talent over the past few years.

Increased Support from Sponsors and Publicity in the Media:

The ever-increasing popularity of women's cricket has caught the interest of many media networks as well as corporate sponsors. The financial potential of the sport of cricket has been substantially improved as a result of major corporations and brands signing sponsorship deals with female cricket players. In addition, there has been an increase in the amount of coverage provided by the media, with matches played both domestically and internationally receiving more broadcast, live streaming, and analysis.

Changing the Way We Think About Gender:

The rise of women's cricket in India has not only contributed to the game's popularity on the field, but it has also helped to reshape the conventional gender standards that prevail in the country. Female cricketers have emerged as potent icons of drive, shattering preconceived notions and motivating millions of young girls to achieve their ambitions, whether in the realm of sports or another. Women's cricket has sent a powerful message of gender equality and empowerment by showing that women can flourish in a sport that was traditionally dominated by males. This is a significant step toward achieving gender parity in sports.

The Opportunities and the Challenges:

Even though it has gone a long way, women's cricket in India is still facing a number of obstacles. There is still controversy around the salary disparity between male and female cricket players. There is a significant pay gap between male and female cricket players, despite the fact that the women's team has made amazing progress in recent years. The fight for equal pay and recognition is one that will carry on for some time, but it has picked up steam over the past few years.

In addition, there is a demand for additional improvements to be made to the infrastructure and facilities that are offered to female cricket players, particularly at the grassroots level. It will be essential to invest in infrastructure, training, and coaching facilities for women's cricket if the sport is to continue its rapid expansion in the coming years.

Perspectives for the Future:

There is reason to be optimistic about the future of women's cricket in India. It appears that the sport is going to continue to thrive given the increased attention, support, and passion that has been shown for it. The depth of potential in the country is shown by the rise of young athletes like Shafali Verma, Smriti Mandhana, and Deepti Sharma, who have made their mark on the international stage.

It is anticipated that the Women's T20 Challenge, which is a competition that is held as part of the IPL, would continue to expand and become a more prominent stage on which female cricket players from India and around the world may display their talents. Additionally, the creation of additional bilateral series, including multi-format series, will be vital to maintain the interest in women's cricket and provide players with plenty opportunities to compete at the top level. This will be the case if the goal is to provide players with ample opportunities to play at the greatest level.

The progression of women's cricket in India is a monument to the passion, talent, and perseverance of the players who have broken traditional gender standards in order to achieve success in the sport.

It is a tale of passion, dedication, and success that has reimagined the roles that women are expected to play in Indian culture and served as an inspiration to a new generation of young women. The future of women's cricket in India appears to be bright, and the sport has the potential to scale even higher heights over the next few years, despite the fact that there are obstacles that need to be overcome and problems that need to be solved. Not only has women's cricket in India established itself as a dominant force in the world of sports, but it has also become a symbol of female empowerment and equality in a country that is in the process of rewriting its own narrative.

2.2 Inspirational stories of female cricketers

Female cricketers from around the world have battled the odds, smashed prejudices, and reached to the top of their sport. As a result, they have become motivational role models for aspiring athletes, particularly young girls. These women have not only proved their extraordinary aptitude for the game of cricket, but they have also demonstrated an unrelenting tenacity, resiliency, and a passion for the sport. In this essay, we will look at the lives of a few great female cricket players who have made an unforgettable imprint on the game as well as on society. These women have broken barriers and inspired generations.

1. **Mithali Raj, often known as "The Captain Cool":**

   A legendary figure in the sport of women's cricket, Mithali Raj served as the skipper of the Indian women's cricket team for many years. Because of the cool and collected way in which she plays the game, people often refer to her as "Captain Cool." Mithali is the first female cricketer in history to score 7,000 runs in One Day Internationals (ODIs), and she holds the record for most runs scored in women's One Day Internationals (ODIs).

   When Mithali was a small child, she was motivated to pursue a career in cricket by the ambitions of her brother, who was also a cricket player. She made her debut on the international stage when she was 16 years old and came to stardom quite quickly. However, she did not have an easy road ahead of her because she had to overcome several obstacles and societal expectations that questioned her decision to participate in a traditionally male-dominated sport. Her journey was everything from straightforward.

The narrative of Mithali serves as a powerful illustration of her persistent dedication and commitment to the sport. She has been a staunch supporter of women's cricket and has persistently worked to ensure that female cricket players in India have equal recognition and opportunity. Her path can serve as a source of motivation for young women with lofty goals to shatter stereotypes, flourish in their chosen fields of study, and become leaders in their communities.

2. **Ellyse Perry, author of "The Dual International":**

The name Ellyse Perry is famous in the sport of cricket with both variety and skill. She is an Australian athlete that competes on the international stage in both cricket and soccer, and she represents her country in both of those sports. Perry made her first appearance for the Australian women's cricket team when she was 16 years old. She soon established herself as one of the best all-rounders in the world after her debut.

The fact that Perry was able to achieve the highest levels of success in not one but two different sports is what makes her tale so motivational. Her devotion, work ethic, and intense love for the sports of cricket and soccer have made her a great role model for young athletes all around the world. The path that Perry has traveled teaches us that with the appropriate attitude and a strong will, anyone can achieve greatness in a number of different fields.

3. **Overcoming Anxiety, by Sarah Taylor:**

Not only is English wicketkeeper and batswoman Sarah Taylor known for her talent in the game of cricket, but also for her bravery in overcoming anxiety throughout her career. She is well-known for her excellent glovework and beautiful batting, both of which she displayed while she was a member of the England women's cricket team.

The fact that Sarah was so candid about her battles with anxiety, which ultimately resulted in her stepping away from cricket to concentrate on her mental well-being, makes her tale a source of motivation. Her openness to discuss the difficulties she faced was essential in breaking the silence that surrounded mental health issues in the sporting world. A victory over hardship, Sarah's comeback to the competition served as a powerful illustration of the significance of making one's mental health a top priority.

4. **Smriti Mandhana, the Brightest Star in the Making:**

Smriti Mandhana, a cricketer from India, has quickly established herself as one of the most promising young players in women's cricket. Her deft strokeplay and reliable performances have earned her praise and admiration from tennis fans all around the world. The enthusiasm that her older brother had for the game of cricket piqued Smriti's interest in the sport at an early age.

The story of how she went from living in a village in Maharashtra to being a famous performer all over the world is one that may teach us a lot about dedication and perseverance. Smriti's achievements have not only garnered her personal acclaim, but they have also inspired a large number of young women in India to pursue their aspirations of becoming cricket players. Her life serves as an example of how talent, perseverance, and dedication may bring one closer to realizing one's ambitions.

5. **Stafanie Taylor, who is setting a good example for the West Indies:**
   The West Indies women's cricket team, which is captained by Stafanie Taylor, has been a driving force in the promotion of women's cricket throughout the Caribbean. She is well-known for her dynamic all-round ability and has been an essential contributor to the ascent to prominence in West Indian cricket.

   The story of Stafanie's rise from modest beginnings in Jamaica to the position of head of state in her country is an uplifting example of endurance and resilience. She has been a continuous advocate for increased funding and opportunities for women's cricket in the West Indies, serving as a model for political and business leaders in other countries that play cricket. The life of Stafanie exemplifies the power that a single, self-motivated person can have in determining the course of events for the future of women's sports in their nation.

6. **Lisa Sthalekar, a forerunner in the field of medicine in Australia:**
   Former Australian cricketer and trailblazer Lisa Sthalekar was instrumental in the development of women's cricket. She was an exciting all-rounder who made substantial contributions to Australia's domination in the sport during her career. Her story is a demonstration of perseverance, tenacity, and the ability to adapt and flourish in a competitive environment that is constantly shifting and changing.

   Lisa's achievements are not limited to her playing career; in addition, she is well-known in the cricket community for her work as a commentator and as an advocate for women's cricket. Her motivational narrative exemplifies the potential for players to become ambassadors for their respective sports and to be agents of constructive change.

7. **The Power-Hitter Harmanpreet Kaur comes in at number seven.**
   Harmanpreet Kaur, the vice-captain of the Indian women's cricket team, is well-known for her aggressive batting and power-hitting ability on the cricket pitch. Her unforgettable performance in the semi-final of the Women's World Cup in 2017, in which she scored an explosive hundred, won her attention all over the world.

   The journey that Harmanpreet has taken so far has been one of overcoming obstacles, particularly when she was forced to pick between following her passion for cricket and sticking to the standards of society. Her remarkable journey to the top of the Indian cricket scene exemplifies the capacity of individuals to defy conventional norms and doggedly pursue their goals in spite of the obstacles that may lie in their way.

8. **Charlotte Edwards, a Leader Who Has Served for a Very Long Time:**
Charlotte Edwards is regarded as one of the most influential figures in women's cricket, having served as the previous captain of the England women's cricket team. Her leadership on and off the field has left an indelible stamp on the women's game, and it would be impossible to erase it.

The narrative of Charlotte exemplifies dedication, as she held the position of captain for more than a decade and guided England to a number of notable triumphs during that time. Because of her commitment to cricket and her ability to motivate the other players on her team, she has become a model for young players who are interested in the sport. This demonstrates the significance of leadership in competitive sports.

9. **Meg Lanning, an icon of our contemporary era:**
Meg Lanning, the captain of the Australian women's cricket team, is widely regarded as a pioneering figure in the field of women's cricket in the modern era. She always performs to a high standard and has the capacity to guide her team to success. Meg's journey is a reflection of her unrelenting pursuit of perfection, and she continues to motivate young athletes to set high expectations for themselves thanks to the example she has established.

10. **Shafali Verma, also known as The Young Sensation:**

The Indian opening batter Shafali Verma has wreaked havoc in the world of cricket with her daring approach and aggressive style of play. She made her debut on the international stage when she was just 15 years old and rapidly became a phenomenon in the world of cricket. The transformational potential of skill and perseverance is demonstrated by Shafali's remarkable journey from a small town in Haryana to representing India at the highest level.

The extraordinary talent, dogged persistence, and unflappable spirit of these pioneering female cricketers from around the world are on full display in these motivational accounts of their journeys in the sport, which have earned them the title of role models. They have broken down barriers and redefined what is possible in the world of athletics, and their adventures serve as a source of motivation and support for young women who aspire to have successful athletic careers. Each of these women has left an indelible mark on the history of cricket, and they continue to inspire the next generation of cricket players by demonstrating that the sky is the limit for those who aren't afraid to dream big and put in a lot of hard effort to achieve their ambitions. Their anecdotes not only add to the rich legacy of women's cricket but also make a significant contribution to the overarching narrative of women's empowerment and equal treatment in society.

2.3 Impact of women's cricket on gender perceptions in India

Cricket, a sport that is so popular in India that it is often compared to a religion, has a long history of being linked to the aggressiveness and predominance of men. In spite of this, women's cricket in India has been on an ascent over the better part of the last two decades, making considerable achievements in terms of performance, visibility, and influence. The rise of women's cricket has not only altered the competitive environment, but it has also had a significant influence on how people in this country think about gender roles. In this essay, we will investigate the numerous ways in which women's cricket in India has challenged old gender conventions, transformed views, and contributed to greater gender equality. Specifically, we will focus on the impact that this sport has had on the Indian subcontinent.

1. **Subverting Assumptions Regarding Gender:**
   The development of women's cricket in India has posed a challenge to the strongly ingrained gender preconceptions that have, for a very long time, limited women to particular roles and expectations. Female cricketers have demonstrated that women are capable of excelling in cricket, a sport that has traditionally been dominated by men. This has destroyed the idea that cricket is primarily a male activity, which was prevalent in a society in which cricket was played. Their outstanding performances on the field have demonstrated that a player's level of talent, dedication, and passion for the game are not contingent on their gender.

2. **Motivating Today's Young Women:**
   The women's cricket league in India serves as a source of motivation and encouragement for young women all around the country, which is one of the sport's most significant consequences. When young girls witness their female cricketing idols compete, they see living proof that they, too, are capable of dreaming big and achieving their goals, despite what society expects of them. Mithali Raj, Harmanpreet Kaur, and Smriti Mandhana are just a few of the female cricketers who have become role models for young girls and have inspired a new generation of young women to take up the sport of cricket and pursue their aspirations with self-assurance.

3. **Visibility and representation are the third point.**
   The growing visibility of women's cricket has been an important factor in the shift toward new perspectives. Significant viewership has been attracted as a result of the broadcasting of women's matches both internationally and domestically, as well as high-profile competitions like the Women's World Cup. The role that the media has had in providing female cricketers with equal attention and respect has helped to a shift in attitudes regarding gender. Cricket for women is no longer on the margins; rather, it has established itself as an important part of the national sports narrative.

4. **Discussions on the Issue of Equal Pay:**
   The growing importance of women's cricket has generated conversations regarding gender equality in sports, notably in regard to salary inequalities between male and female athletes. Female cricketers have been having a discourse about equal pay, which has led to changes in the landscape of cricket as a result of the conversation. Despite the fact that discrepancies still remain, this issue has been brought to light, which has produced a consciousness that continues to promote change.

5. **Autonomy Achieved Through Athletic Participation:**
   Cricket has been instrumental in the empowerment of women in India by opening doors to opportunities for the women's personal development, educational pursuits, and professional advancement. Through their participation in cricket, a significant number of female athletes have been able to advance their studies and secure work. This empowerment extends to their families and communities, promoting a bigger narrative of gender equality in the process.

6. **The Effect on Conventional Ways of Thinking:**
   The sport of women's cricket has been instrumental in the transformation of conventional ideas inside the homes and communities of India. This has thrown a wrench into the widely held beliefs that males should take the lead in athletic endeavors and that women should focus on their responsibilities at home. The accomplishments of female cricket players have turned into a source of pride for their families, their communities, and the nation as a whole.

7. **Increasing the Number of People Who Play Sports:**
   The achievements of the women's cricket team have had a trickle-down effect, increasing the number of women who participate in sports generally. Young women are breaking down the obstacles that once prevented them from participating in a variety of sports. This is a positive development. Schools and sports academies have started investing more money in girls' sports programs, which provides females with equal opportunity to develop their athletic skills.

8. **The Effects on Culture and Society:**
   In India, cricket has never been merely a sport; rather, it has always been a significant part of the country's culture. This cultural narrative has been enriched as a result of the rise of women's cricket, which has contributed to a society that is more diverse and inclusive. Female cricket players are held in high esteem for their accomplishments, and the game itself has developed into a wellspring of community pride and cohesiveness.

9. **Initiatives to Achieve Gender Parity:**
   The influence of women's cricket extends to several projects and legislation pertaining to gender equality. The importance of sports has been recognized by numerous organizations and authorities, and as a result, efforts have been made to promote gender equality not only in sports but also in a variety of other areas

of life. This includes the implementation of initiatives to close the wage gap between men and women and to give women with equal chances for participation, leadership, and recognition.

10. **The Important Role Played by Cricketing Icons:**
    Female cricket players in India who have achieved iconic status have been crucial in shaping how people think about gender roles. Their behavior both on and off the field, as well as their qualities as leaders, and their dedication to the sport have been motivational. They have leveraged their roles as ambassadors for the game in order to campaign for broader social and gender concerns. In addition, they have used their positions as ambassadors for the game.

11. **The Obstacles in Our Path and the Way Forward:**

In spite of the great effects that women's cricket has had in India, considerable obstacles still need to be overcome. There is still a gap in salary between men and women, and there is opportunity for additional investment in the infrastructure, facilities, and growth of the sport at the grassroots level. Additionally, prejudices and preconceptions have deep roots, and it may take some time to totally remove them from society. However, the trajectory of women's cricket in India is optimistic, and these problems are gradually being addressed in a growing number of ways.

There is no denying the effect that women's cricket has had on the way people in India view gender roles. It has broken down barriers, challenged established norms, and fostered the development of a society that is more egalitarian and welcoming to everyone. Not only have the achievements of female cricketers served as a source of motivation for younger girls, but they have also sparked discussions on the importance of gender equality and the liberation of women. The rise of women's cricket is a testament to the transformative potential of sports in defying preconceived notions and influencing the views of society as a whole. As women's cricket continues to develop, it will play a crucial part in molding the future of gender attitudes in India. This will pave the way for greater equality and empowerment for women and girls in the country.

Chapter 3

Cricket and Caste Dynamics

Cricket, sometimes known as the "gentleman's game," is more than simply a sport in India; it is a cultural phenomenon that brings millions of people from all parts of the country together. Cricket is praised for its capacity to bring people together from a variety of different walks of life; but, the sport also reflects and, at times, even influences the intricate social structures that exist. The caste system in India is an example of one component of society that has intersected with cricket. The caste system is a social structure that is highly embedded and historically rooted in India. This essay investigates the complex link that exists between cricket and the caste system in India. It does so by analyzing the historical context, the function of caste in cricket, and the influence that cricket has had on people's conceptions of caste.

1. **Contextualization Historique:**
   The beginnings of cricket in India can be traced back to the time of British colonial rule. During this time, the British elite were responsible for the sport's introduction and development in India. Cricket was largely played by British soldiers and bureaucrats, and participation in the sport was frequently restricted on the basis of social class and racial identity. Because of the sport's steadily growing popularity, these restrictions were eventually lifted, and high-class Indian citizens were able to take part in the competition.
   The first known game of cricket was played in India in 1721 in Cambay, Gujarat, between British sailors and local inhabitants. The game was played by British sailors. However, due to the British colonialists' dominance of cricket, early Indian participation was restricted, and the wealthy were the only ones who could afford to play the game and promote it.
2. **The Development of Clubs Based on Caste:**
   The Parsi community played a pioneering role when cricket began to acquire popularity among Indians, particularly in Bombay (now Mumbai) and the western portion of the country. This was especially true in Bombay. In the year

1848, a group of Parsis in Bombay established the Oriental Cricket Club, which is often regarded as the moment when Indians first became actively involved in the sport. This was a key step in undermining the British domination of cricket and opening up opportunities for fans of Indian cricket.

The caste system was further mirrored in the establishment of cricket clubs and groups that were based on the caste system. The Parsis, Hindus, Muslims, and Europeans all competed against one another in a significant cricket event known as the Bombay Quadrangular. This competition was held in Bombay. This event not only stoked the fires of regional animosity but also highlighted the ways in which caste and cricket connect, with distinct communities being represented by their respective teams.

3. **The Influence of the Parsis and the Early Indian Pioneers:**
   The Parsis were among the first to play a significant part in the sport of cricket in India. Prominent players such as Khurshedji Rustomji Cama, Sorabji Pochkhanawala, and Dinshaw Wacha were among the first to make significant contributions to the game's formative years. These individuals bucked the limits that were imposed on them by the caste system and established themselves as influential characters in the world of cricket. Their efforts helped pave the path for increased engagement in the sport among Indians.

4. **A Cricket Match Between the Maharaja of Patiala's Team and the All-India Cricket Team:**
   In 1892, the All-India cricket team, which was headed by the Maharaja of Patiala, set out on a tour of England. During their time there, they left a profound impression on the cricketing establishment in England. This trip was a significant achievement since it proved that Indians are capable of competing successfully on an international level. The removal of caste-based restrictions and the establishment of a more welcoming atmosphere in cricket were both furthered by the recruitment of Indian players from a variety of ethnic and socioeconomic backgrounds for the team.

5. **The establishment of the Board of Control for Cricket in India (BCCI)**
   In December of 1928, the Board of Control for Cricket in India (BCCI) was founded, and it quickly rose to the position of being the regulating authority for cricket throughout the country. A defining point in the history of Indian cricket was the establishment of the Board of Control for Cricket in India (BCCI), which aimed to standardize the game and provide order to the otherwise disorganized structure of cricket administration.

   Even though the Board of Control for Cricket in India was a monumental step forward for Indian cricket, the organization was not without its fair share of caste-based politics and power battles inside its ranks. The administration of cricket was influenced by caste-based connections and alliances, which exemplified how social factors may permeate all facets of the sport's organizational structure.

6. **The Selection of Players and Castes:**
Caste dynamics have also been shown to have an impact on player selection at times, with some selectors and team managers showing a preference for players from their own communities. However, such prejudices have been the subject of debate and criticism, and there have been ongoing efforts to guarantee that the selection of players is based on merit rather than caste-based favoritism.

7. **Icons Hailing from a Variety of Cultural Traditions:**
The sport of cricket in India has seen the rise of famous players from a variety of backgrounds. These players, such as Sachin Tendulkar, Rahul Dravid, and Anil Kumble, have transcended caste and regional affiliations in order to become legends in the sport of cricket. Regardless of where they came from in the caste system, the general public recognizes and admires these players for their achievements.

8. **Representation of Castes and Regions in the Eighth Chapter:**
In Indian cricket, caste and regional loyalties have frequently intersected, which has had the effect of shaping the way different regions are represented. There is a possibility that more players hailing from states with a robust cricketing tradition will be selected to play for the national side. This may give the appearance of regional favoritism. These regional affiliations are frequently entangled with caste dynamics, as it is possible that certain locations have a higher proportion of particular castes than others.

9. **The Influence of Caste on the Infrastructure and Facilities of Cricket:**
The growth of cricket facilities and infrastructure has also been influenced, to a certain extent, by the social dynamics of caste. It's possible that politics based on caste may cause certain areas to receive more money and attention than others, which could result in the improvement of cricket facilities in certain areas. This, in turn, might result to a concentration of talent from specific regions, which can damage the sport of Indian cricket's overall balance.

10. **Difficulties and Issues of Controversy:**
In spite of the great progress that has been made, problems connected to caste and cricket still exist. It is possible for unconscious and explicit prejudices and biases based on caste to still have an effect on opportunities and recognition within the sport. Subtle forms of prejudice and discrimination frequently go untreated because of their insidious nature.

11. **Projects Aimed at Promoting Inclusivity:**
There have been efforts made to expand participation in cricket and to foster an atmosphere in which talent and accomplishment take precedence over other considerations in terms of selection and recognition. Steps have been done by

organizations such as the BCCI to encourage diversity and inclusivity within the sport of cricket.

12. **The Effects That Social Movements Have On Society:**
The way that cricket is played and governed has been shaped, in part, by social movements and campaigns that advocate for social justice and equality. These campaigns have brought attention to discrimination on the basis of caste and the necessity of inclusivity in all facets of life, including sports.

13. **The Function of the Media**
The influence that the media has on people's perspectives and attitudes is significant. The way
in which the media covers cricket has the potential to either reinforce or challenge preconceived notions based on caste. The responsibility to encourage diversity and inclusiveness in their reporting on the sport is on the shoulders of media companies.

14. **Icons and Role Models for Young People:**
It is possible for prominent players and cricketing icons to change people's perspectives and attitudes toward the sport. They have the potential to make a significant impact on their fans and following, which in turn contributes to beneficial changes in society, when they advocate for inclusiveness and equality.

15. **Moving in the Right Direction:**

Even while cricket in India has made considerable efforts toward becoming more inclusive and based on merit, there is still a lot of room for improvement in these areas. Everyone involved in cricket—its administrators, players, fans, and other stakeholders—has some say in the direction the game will go in the future and how it will interact with caste dynamics. Cricket has the potential to act as a platform for the promotion of unity, diversity, and inclusivity as the nation continues to develop. It can do this by transcending the bounds of caste and contributing to a society that is more egalitarian.

The relationship between caste dynamics in India and the game of cricket is a complicated one, as it is impacted by historical legacies, cultural attitudes, and modern concerns. Cricket has been a vehicle for challenging caste norms and providing opportunities to brilliant individuals regardless of their origin. Despite these positive effects, the sport has also been plagued by internal caste-based politics and biases.

The joint efforts of stakeholders, including administrators, players, and fans, in encouraging diversity, inclusivity, and equitable chances for all will have a significant impact on the trajectory of cricket's future in India. Cricket, a great cultural force in India, has the ability to lead the way in dismantling barriers based on caste and contribute to the creation of a society that is more egalitarian and welcoming to those of all backgrounds.

3.1 The intersection of cricket and caste in Indian society

The caste system in India is highly rooted, and cricket has a strange and complicated relationship with it. Cricket is frequently compared to a religion in India. The sport, which is played all over the world regardless of social standing or location, has been used both as a mirror to reflect caste issues and as a stage upon which to confront them. This essay digs into the delicate confluence of caste and cricket in Indian society. It investigates the historical context, the importance of caste in player selection, the impact on player careers, as well as the ongoing challenges and developments in this complicated relationship.

1. **Contextualization Historique:**
   The influence of British colonialism on the development of cricket in India can't be separated from that influence. After its introduction by the British in the 18th century, the sport quickly rose to prominence as a favorite pleasure activity for colonial administrators and soldiers. Initially, only the most affluent members of British society could play cricket, and other Indians were barred from participating entirely because of the social order that prevailed at the time.

2. **The Original Trailblazers:**
   The members of the Parsi community in Bombay, which is now known as Mumbai, were extremely influential in the formative years of cricket in India. The Parsis established the Oriental Cricket Club in 1848, which was a pivotal moment in the history of Indian participation in the game of cricket. Because of this advancement, members of the Parsi community were finally able to break down boundaries and join in cricket, despite the fact that they were subject to some degree of scrutiny from society.

3. **The Caste-Based Teams and the Bombay Quadrangular Teams:**
   In the early 20th century, a famous cricket competition called the Bombay Quadrangular was contested. This tournament is credited with introducing caste dynamics into the world of cricket. There were four teams competing in the competition, each representing a distinct community: the Parsis, the Hindus, the Muslims, and the Europeans. Even though it was supposed to be a battle between different regions, it invariably showed how caste and cricket are intertwined, with different communities being represented by different teams.

4. **The Position of the Maharaja of Patiala in Society:**
   The All-India Cricket Team, which was being captained by the Maharaja of Patiala at the time, set sail for England in the year 1892. This tour was notable because it challenged the prejudices that had limited the involvement of Indian players based on their caste or social background. These stereotypes had hampered the involvement of Indian players in the past and this tour indicated that they could compete at an international level.

5. **The establishment of the Cricket Board of Control in India (BCCI):**
   In 1928, the Board of Control for Cricket in India (BCCI) was founded, and it

quickly rose to the position of being the governing authority for cricket throughout the country. An important turning point in the history of Indian cricket was the establishment of the Board of Control for Cricket in India (BCCI), which aimed to standardize the game and bring order to the otherwise disorganized landscape of cricket administration. In spite of this, caste-based connections and alliances continued to play a part in the administration of cricket, which had an effect on the power dynamics and decision-making processes.

6. **The Selection of Players and Castes:**
   There have been instances where the caste system has been used to choose players in Indian cricket. There have been charges that selectors and team management have shown favoritism toward players from their own communities, which has led to accusations of favoritism based on caste. Controversy and criticism have arisen as a result of these prejudices, regardless of whether they are actual or perceived.

7. **Disparities in Representation Based on Region:**
   In Indian cricket, caste and regional loyalties have frequently intersected, which has had the effect of shaping the way different regions are represented. It's possible that states with robust cricketing cultures will have a greater number of players on the national squad, which could give the appearance of regional favoritism. These regional affiliations are frequently entangled with caste dynamics, as it is possible that certain locations have a higher proportion of particular castes than others.

8. **Discrimination Away From the Playing Field and Other Obstacles:**
   Even though the dynamics of caste have less direct impact on the careers of players in modern sports, off-field prejudice and biases can still have an impact on opportunities and recognition in the industry. Both overt and covert discrimination can have a long-lasting effect on a player's career and the opportunities that lie ahead for their future.

9. **Projects Aimed at Promoting Inclusivity:**
   There have been efforts made to expand participation in cricket and to foster an atmosphere in which talent and accomplishment take precedence over other considerations in terms of selection and recognition. Steps have been done by organizations such as the BCCI to encourage diversity and inclusivity within the sport of cricket.

10. **The Function of the Media:**
    The influence that the media has on people's perspectives and attitudes is significant. The way in which the media covers cricket has the potential to either reinforce or challenge preconceived notions based on caste. The responsibility to encourage diversity and inclusiveness in their reporting on the sport is on the shoulders of media companies.

11. **Iconic Figures and Role Models:**
    It is possible for prominent players and cricketing icons to change people's perspectives and attitudes toward the sport. They have the potential to make a significant impact on their fans and following, which in turn contributes to beneficial changes in society, when they advocate for inclusiveness and equality.

12. **Difficulties and Debates Concerning:**
    In spite of the great progress that has been made, problems connected to caste and cricket still exist. It is possible for unconscious and explicit prejudices and biases based on caste to still have an effect on opportunities and recognition within the sport. Subtle forms of prejudice and discrimination frequently go untreated because of their insidious nature.

13. **The Effects That Social Movements Have On Society:**
    The way that cricket is played and governed has been shaped, in part, by social movements and campaigns that advocate for social justice and equality. These campaigns have brought attention to discrimination on the basis of caste and the necessity of inclusivity in all facets of life, including sports.

14. **Moving in the Right Direction:**

Even while cricket in India has made considerable efforts toward becoming more inclusive and based on merit, there is still a lot of room for improvement in these areas. Everyone involved in cricket—its administrators, players, fans, and other stakeholders—has some say in the direction the game will go in the future and how it will interact with caste dynamics. Cricket has the potential to act as a platform for the promotion of unity, diversity, and inclusivity as the nation continues to develop. It can do this by transcending the bounds of caste and contributing to a society that is more egalitarian.

The relationship between caste and cricket in Indian society is intricate and has complex origins that run deep in the sport's long and illustrious history. Cricket has both mirrored and opposed the dynamics of caste throughout its history, and it continues to play an important part in shaping the attitudes and perceptions of society. The joint efforts of stakeholders, including administrators, players, and fans, in encouraging diversity, inclusivity, and equitable chances for all will have a significant impact on the trajectory of cricket's future in India. Cricket, a great cultural force in India, has the ability to lead the way in dismantling barriers based on caste and contribute to the creation of a society that is more egalitarian and welcoming to those of all backgrounds.

3.2 Success stories of cricketers from marginalized castes

Cricket, which is sometimes lauded as the heart and soul of India, has been a fantastic platform for individuals from a variety of backgrounds, especially those from oppressed castes, to climb to prominence. Although the early history of the sport was marked by the supremacy of the British elite, the sport has since evolved into an arena where talent and skill often prevail above social hierarchies. This contrasts with the early history of the sport, which was marked by the dominance of the British elite. This essay examines the motivational success stories of cricket players from underrepresented castes who have defied societal odds, achieved great heights in the sport, and become role models for millions of people. These individuals have defied societal odds, achieved great heights in the sport, and become role models for millions of people.

1. **Vinod Kambli, also known as "The Left-Handed Maverick":**
   Former Indian cricketer Vinod Kambli is a spectacular example of skill rising from poor origins. He was one of India's most successful players. Kambli comes from a Dalit family, and the fact that he was able to make it all the way from the small alleys of Mumbai's slums to the biggest platform in cricket speaks volumes about his exceptional talent. Legend has it that Kambli and Sachin Tendulkar played together back when they were students at the same school. After graduating, Kambli went on to make his debut for the Indian national side in the 1990s.

   Incredible batting performances characterized Kambli's career, one of the highlights of which being a record-breaking partnership with Sachin Tendulkar in a school cricket tournament. His career, however, was plagued by scandals and challenges despite the early success he enjoyed in his field. However, the fact that he rose from obscurity to become a prominent figure in cricket continues to serve as motivation for young players who come from families with similar socioeconomic backgrounds.

2. **The Spin Wizard, Erapalli Prasanna, comes in at number two.**
   Erapalli Prasanna, a pioneering cricketer who came from a Dalit household, is considered to be one of the best spin bowlers India has ever produced. Prasanna overcame many obstacles during his formative years despite having been born in Bangalore in 1940. However, his remarkable abilities as a spinner are what brought him widespread recognition on a global scale.

   The ability to outwit batters with spin and guile was what set Prasanna apart as a player throughout his career. He was a crucial contributor to India's historic victory in the series against England in 1971. Not only did his achievements as a cricket player bring respect to his skills, but they also showed that members of less privileged castes could achieve success in the sport.

3. **Kedar Jadhav, who is known as "The All-Rounder":**
   Kedar Jadhav is a Maratha all-rounder who plays cricket on the international stage for India. His family is originally from the state of Maharashtra. Growing up, he had to overcome a number of obstacles, including difficult financial circumstances; yet, his unshakeable perseverance and natural talent for cricket paved the road for his success.

   The life of Jadhav is a modern-day example of a cricket player who came from a disadvantaged background yet managed to carve out a niche for himself on the international scene. The Indian cricket team has benefited tremendously from his energetic performances both at the crease and behind the bowling machine.

4. **Eknath Solkar, known as "The Fielding Maestro":**
Eknath Solkar was a talented cricketer recognized for his remarkable fielding skills. He played a variety of positions on the field. He belonged to the Adivasi community and had a modest upbringing to go along with it. Solkar was regarded as one of the best fielders in the history of the game due to his acrobatic fielding, which gained him a reputation for being instrumental in India's victory over England in the Test series that took place in 1971.

Solkar's path, which started in the rural areas of Maharashtra's tribal people, is illustrative of the possibility for individuals from underrepresented populations to reach greatness in the sport of cricket. His name will forever be remembered as a legend in the annals of Indian cricket history.

5. **Rajinder Goel, also known as "The Unsung Hero":**
Left-arm spinner Rajinder Goel, who was a member of a community that was historically oppressed, was regarded as one of the most successful bowlers in the history of first-class cricket. In spite of the fact that he did not play much cricket at the international level, he was a consistent performer in the domestic circuit and racked up an astonishing number of wickets.

The narrative of Goel is a demonstration of the tenacity and commitment of cricket players who may not have achieved worldwide stardom but have left an everlasting impression on the domestic circuit. His achievement is a source of motivation for those individuals who follow their enthusiasm for the game with unwavering dedication.

6. **Ramesh Powar, also known as "The Off-Spin Dynamo":**
Cricket player Ramesh Powar, who hails from Maharashtra in India, is famous for his off-spin bowling style. His rise from a humble beginning to a position of prominence for India in international cricket is a testament to his dogged determination and tireless effort.

Power's career was defined by his unwavering commitment to the game, and he made significant contributions to the sport both as a bowler and as a lower-order batsman. The fact that he was able to achieve success despite the challenges he faced is an inspiration to others who come from disadvantaged backgrounds and want to be successful in cricket.

7. **Pravin Amre, sometimes known as "The Technical Genius":**
Pravin Amre, a cricketer with Marathi ancestry, was lauded for his technically proficient batting style. He established himself as a star in both the domestic and international arenas of cricket by showcasing extraordinary talent and dogged drive.

Amre's rise from the slums of Mumbai's chawls to the position of representing India at the highest level is a testament to his brilliance as well as his tenacity.

His achievements have served as a source of motivation for a whole generation of up-and-coming cricket players who have their sights set on winning it all.

8. **Arun Lal, who calls himself "The Resilient Opener":**
   Arun Lal was a resilient opening batsman for the Indian cricket team. He was a cricket player who came from a disadvantaged community. He demonstrated great determination and skill despite the fact that he was battling illness as well as various hurdles throughout his career.

   The narrative of Lal exemplifies the qualities of bravery and perseverance in the face of

   adversity. His victorious cricketing career acts as motivation for those who must persevere through challenges and difficulties in order to realize their goals in the sport.

9. **Bhagwat Chandrasekhar, the legendary leg-spin player:**
   The leg-spinner Bhagwat Chandrasekhar, who came from a disadvantaged family, was an important player in the history of spin bowling in Indian cricket. Because of his leg-spin and his ability to confound batters with it, he established himself as a fearsome opponent in international cricket.

   The path that Chandrasekhar took from a rural community in Karnataka to the forefront of international cricket is illustrative of the extraordinary potential that exists among cricket players who come from underprivileged backgrounds. His achievements in the game of cricket in India are still celebrated to this day.

10. **R Ashwin, also known as The Contemporary Star:**

Ravichandran Ashwin is a current cricketer who comes from a Brahmin family and is widely considered to be one of the best spin spinners in India. The fact that he rose from a household that was considered to be middle-class to international prominence exemplifies the merit-based ethos of modern cricket.

Ashwin's success, both as a spinner and as a lower-order batsman, serves as a testament to the inclusivity of modern cricket, which places a primary emphasis on talent and performance as the key criteria for recognition.

The achievements of Indian cricket players who come from underrepresented castes are illustrative of the power that skill, determination, and perseverance have in overcoming the limitations imposed by society. Not only have these cricketers attained excellence in the game, but they have also established themselves as role models for young players coming from comparable environments. Their experiences encourage people from underprivileged backgrounds to follow their goals, and they show that cricket, which is frequently viewed as a sport that provides an equal playing field, may in fact serve as a stage on which talent can be showcased, regardless of a person's socioeconomic or caste background. These anecdotes serve as a reminder of the transformative potential that sports have in terms of questioning the conventions of society and empowering individuals to shoot for the stars.

3.3 Initiatives to promote inclusivity in cricket

Cricket, a sport that is immensely popular in a lot of different places throughout the world, has the ability to bring people together regardless of their race, class, or nationality. Cricket, however, has struggled with issues with diversity and inclusivity, much like many other fields of endeavor have done. In recent years, there has been a rising realization of the need to promote inclusivity in cricket in order to guarantee that the sport continues to be a welcome and accessible arena for everyone. This goal is intended to ensure that cricket will continue to be played by people of all backgrounds. This essay explores the numerous measures that have been done to develop inclusivity in the world of cricket. These initiatives include addressing issues of gender inequity, fostering diversity, and eradicating discrimination. The essay also explores the various activities that have been taken to promote diversity.

1. **The Revolution of Women in Cricket:**
   The campaign for gender equality and the promotion of women's cricket has been one of the most important and game-changing movements in cricket. Throughout its history, women's cricket has frequently been overlooked and has gotten a significantly lower level of attention and investment than men's cricket has. However, during the course of the last ten years, there has been a revolution in women's cricket, which has resulted in a rise in the number of possibilities available, improved facilities, and increasing recognition.

   Tournaments such as the Women's Big Bash League (WBBL) in Australia, the Women's Indian Premier League (IPL) in India, and the Kia Super League in England are all excellent instances of how the standing of women's cricket has improved as a result of their existence. These leagues not only offer competitive chances, but they also act as platforms to promote women's cricket and give role models for female cricket players who are interested in pursuing a career in the sport.

2. **Financial Parity in the Prize Pool:**
   Cricket's governing bodies and organizations have taken action to address the wage disparity between men and women in the sport. In recent years, efforts have been made to guarantee that female cricketers get prize money and match fees that are comparable to those received by their male counterparts. One important step toward gender equality in sports was taken when the International Cricket Council (ICC) decided to provide the same amount of prize money to the winners of the men's and women's Twenty20 World Cups.

3. **The Participation of Transgender Athletes :**
   The adoption of transgender player inclusion policies by cricket's governing bodies represents a significant advance toward the sport's goal of greater inclusivity. Individuals are now able to participate in cricket based on their gender

identity after the International Cricket Council (ICC) in 2019 approved guidelines for the inclusion of transgender players in the international game.

4. **Programs of Service to the Community:**
A wide variety of cricket organizations and clubs have initiated community outreach programs in an effort to broaden the demographics of people who can participate in the sport. Children and young people who might not otherwise have access to the game are the target audience for these initiatives, which attempt to offer them with coaching, facilities, and opportunities to play. Not only do these projects encourage diversity, but they also seek out and cultivate talent originating from a variety of backgrounds.

5. **Initiatives for Disabled Cricket Players:**
The sport of cricket is no longer restricted to only those with able bodies. The sport of disability cricket, which comprises players with both physical and intellectual limitations, is receiving increased attention thanks to the establishment of several promotional initiatives. Disability cricket programs have been formed by several organizations, such as the England and Wales Cricket Board (ECB). These programs give players with impairments the opportunity to compete and flourish in the sport of cricket.

6. **Initiatives to Combat Racism:**
Cricket has been plagued by instances of racial prejudice on occasion, and the sport has been making efforts to resolve these problems. Efforts to combat racism, such as the International Cricket Council's "Say No to Racism" campaign, have been made in an effort to raise awareness and foster a more accepting atmosphere in the sport of cricket.

7. **Festivities Related to Culture:**
The fact that cricket is played all over the world means that its players and supporters come from a wide variety of cultural backgrounds. Cricket matches and events frequently contain cultural celebrations and traditions that reflect the variety of the cricketing community. This is done with the goal of fostering an inclusive environment. For instance, during the Indian Premier League (IPL), players from a variety of countries get together to appreciate each other's cultures. This helps to build a sense of unity and respect among the players from all of the different nations.

8. **Inclusivity for LGBTQ+ People:**
Cricket has also made significant progress toward promoting an inclusive environment for LGBTQ+ people. Several players have come out as members of the LGBTQ+ community, and cricket boards have declared their support for LGBTQ+ fans and players. Within the cricketing community, it is necessary to take these steps in order to create a more welcoming environment for persons who identify as LGBTQ+.

9. **Development Programs at the Grassroots Level:**
The promotion of inclusiveness must begin at the most fundamental level. Cricket boards and organizations have made investments in grassroots development initiatives with the goal of identifying and cultivating talent from a variety of backgrounds. These programs intend to eliminate barriers and make chances equally available to prospective cricket players from all walks of life and all parts of the world, irrespective of socioeconomic standing or geographic location.

10. **Accessibility for Individuals who Suffer from Disabilities:**
People with impairments have been taken into consideration during the design and modification process of cricket stadiums and other amenities. This comprises seating, facilities, and accommodations that are designed to make watching cricket matches pleasurable and accessible for all spectators, regardless of their level of physical ability.

11. **Promoting Mixed-Gender Participation in Cricket:**
Another activity that fosters diversity is playing cricket with players of both sexes. Cricket clubs and schools in several regions of the world have begun to host mixed-gender matches, which enable male and female players to compete against one another. These projects question the conventional gender norms that exist in the sport and work to promote inclusiveness.

12. **Increasing Indigenous Participation in Cricket:**
Cricket has made its way into indigenous communities in nations like Australia, where it has been used as a tool to engage and empower such communities' native populations. The efforts that have been taken to promote indigenous cricket have been beneficial in encouraging inclusivity and creating possibilities.

13. **Tolerance of All Religious Practices**
Cricket acknowledges the spiritual diversity that exists among its players and spectators. The players' religious beliefs have been taken into consideration, and accommodations have been made to suit those practices. For example, players are permitted to wear turbans or headscarves in accordance with their faith.

14. **Becoming Aware of Mental Health:**
The need to raise awareness about mental health and offer help to individuals who may be struggling is something that cricket's governing bodies, teams, and players have all acknowledged and embraced. Cricket helps to foster a more welcoming atmosphere by putting an emphasis on the mental and emotional well-being of all those who participate in the sport.

15. **Inclusion of Individuals with Disabilities in Coaching and Administration:**
Not only have efforts been made to encourage inclusion on the playing field, but also in the positions of coaching and administration, same efforts have been undertaken. The cricketing ecosystem can be made more varied and welcoming for all participants by implementing programs that encourage the participation of people with disabilities in coaching and administrative roles.

16. **Providing an Inclusive Environment for Match Officials:**
    The expansion of inclusivity measures has led to an increase in the number of women and people from varied backgrounds serving as match officials in both international and domestic competitions. This not only provides examples of positive behavior but also encourages more diverse officiating in sports.

17. **Girls' Cricket Programs at the Grassroots Level:**
    Many organizations have started grass-roots programs in order to encourage more young girls to take part in cricket. These programs are designed to familiarize the young girls with the sport, as well as give them opportunity to develop their skills and take part in competitive play.

18. **Initiatives to Raise Public Knowledge and Awareness:**
    Education and awareness campaigns have been launched on a variety of subjects, including gender equality, prejudice, and racism, by various cricket boards, organizations, and players. These efforts attempt to bring about a shift in mentalities and foster a sense of inclusiveness within the cricketing community.

19. **Affirmative Action: (in parentheses)**
    Some cricket boards have instituted affirmative action policies in an effort to increase the number of underrepresented groups, such as underprivileged castes, in positions of administrative and governance responsibility within the sport of cricket.

20. **Inclusivity with Regard to Supporter Engagement:**

The sport of cricket has also understood the significance of fan participation and inclusiveness. Fan zones and activities that are family-friendly and meant to appeal to a wide audience are frequently featured at cricket matches and other types of stadium events.

Cricket has become a more accessible, varied, and equitable sport as a result of actions that have been taken to promote diversity within the sport. These efforts demonstrate a dedication to developing an ecosystem for cricket that places a high emphasis on skill, diversity, and equality.

These initiatives will play a critical role in ensuring that cricket continues to be a welcome and inclusive arena for players, spectators, and stakeholders from all walks of life as the sport continues to progress toward its next stage of development. The key to securing cricket's long-term viability is creating conditions in which participants of all backgrounds and identities may participate and enjoy the sport on an equal footing, regardless of where they came from.

Chapter 4

Cricket and Regional Unity

In India, the sport of cricket, also known as the "gentleman's game," has grown far beyond its roots as only a competitive activity. It has developed into a cultural phenomenon that bridges the gap between the country's many distinct regions. In spite of the linguistic, cultural, and geographical diversity that exists in India, cricket has been an important factor in the development of regional unity. This essay examines the strong connection between the sport of cricket and regional unity in India. It does so by looking at the historical context, the influence of regional identity on the sport, the role of cricketing heroes, and the impact on national consciousness.

1. **Contextualization Historique:**
   During the time of British colonial rule in India, the British upper class were responsible for the sport's introduction and development into what it is today. These events are considered to be the beginning of the cricket tradition in India. The majority of the game was played by British soldiers and bureaucrats, and Indians only had restricted access to the game. Cricket, on the other hand, began to transcend regional borders and establish a common cultural tie among the numerous Indian regions as it increasingly gained popularity over time.

2. **The Impact of a Regional Sense of Identity:**
   The many distinct areas of India, each with its own distinct language, culture, and traditions, have frequently served as a wellspring of national pride and identity for the Indian people. Cricket, despite its status as a national sport, has always recognized and honored these regional differences. The sport gives areas the opportunity to demonstrate their unique abilities, playing styles, and cricketing customs to the world. Fans from all across the country cheer fervently for their home teams and players, which not only helps to strengthen regional identities but also contributes to a widespread passion for the sport on a national level.

3. **Local Cricket Associations in Each Region:**
   The sport of cricket is played across India and is governed by a number of

different regional cricket associations. These associations, which include the Board of Control for Cricket in India (BCCI), the Mumbai Cricket Association (MCA), and the Karnataka State Cricket Association (KSCA), each represent a different region and play an important role in the development of cricket infrastructure, the cultivation of local talent, and the organization of regional tournaments.

4. **Iconic regional teams include the following:**
The Ranji Trophy is considered to be the most prestigious domestic cricket competition in India. It is played by regional teams that represent India's several states and regions. These teams have developed into emblems of regional pride and have been responsible for the development of some of India's most talented cricket players. For instance, the Mumbai cricket team, the Delhi cricket team, and the Karnataka cricket team are all renowned for their significant contributions to Indian cricket and for the pride they have brought to their respective regions.

5. **Rivalries between Different States:**
The competition between different states is an important part of Indian cricket, and it frequently extends beyond the bounds of the playing field. Fans pay close attention to and look forward with great anticipation to matches that feature regional teams competing against one another, such as the one that will take place between Mumbai and Delhi. These competitions foster a sense of teamwork and healthy competition, which in turn contributes to the cohesion of the region and a shared passion for cricket.

6. **Home Fields and the Tradition of the Fan:**
Eden Gardens in Kolkata, Chinnaswamy Stadium in Bangalore, and Wankhede Stadium in Mumbai are just a few examples of the legendary cricketing venues that can be found in each of the regions. These locations have played a pivotal role in the game's history and have evolved into the cultural epicenter of cricket in their respective regions. Cricket helps to weave a tapestry of regional togetherness through its passionate fan culture, different regional chants, and long-standing local traditions.

7. **Notable Figures from the Community:**
Every area has had its share of cricketing greats, people who are lauded not just for their achievements on the field but also for their contributions to the development of a sense of regional pride. Players like as Sachin Tendulkar, who hails from Mumbai, Rahul Dravid, who hails from Karnataka, and Sourav Ganguly, who hails from Bengal, are not only idols of the sport of cricket but also emblems of regional identity.

8. **Tournaments in the Various Regions:**
In addition to the Ranji Trophy, there are a number of other regional events, like as the Duleep Trophy, the Vijay Hazare Trophy, and the Syed Mushtaq Ali

Trophy, that give players the opportunity to compete on behalf of their respective areas and exhibit their skills. In addition to fostering greater togetherness across the area, these tournaments provide a fertile field for the development of national and international cricket players.

9. **Effects on the Collective Conscience of the Nation:**
Cricket not only helps to foster unity across regions, but it also has a significant impact on the development of national consciousness. The success of the Indian cricket team on the world stage has the potential to bring people together from all parts of the country, regardless of regional distinctions. When India won the 1983 Cricket World Cup, the 2007 ICC World Twenty20, and the 2011 Cricket World Cup, it was one of those unforgettable occasions that created a sense of national pride and solidarity that transcended regional connections.

10. **The Indian Premier League, also known as the IPL:**
The Indian Premier League (IPL), a Twenty20 cricket spectacular, is a great example of how regional identities can coexist with national unity. In this league, city-based franchises representing different parts of India compete against one another. These franchises have each created their own distinct fan bases and cultures, which serves to highlight the multifaceted nature of the nation while also making a contribution to a common Indian sense of identity.

11. **The Function of the Media**
Through the sport of cricket, India's many distinct regions are brought closer together through the power of the media, particularly television and other digital channels. Fans from every nook and cranny of the country are certain to be able to feel a connection to the game and their preferred players because to the broad coverage of the sport and the regional language commentary and analysis that is provided.

12. **Cricketing festivals and celebrations include the following:**
In India, festivals are sometimes held to celebrate various sporting events, particularly cricket matches featuring the Indian national team. The boundaries of regions are ignored as people from all across the country congregate in one place to watch and cheer on the squad. These festivities encourage a sense of togetherness as well as a collective excitement for the sport.

13. **Projects for the Advancement of Regional Development:**
Cricket's governing bodies and associations have come to realize the significance of cultivating talent from a variety of geographical areas. They have ensured that cricket's expansion is both inclusive and widespread by launching development programs, training facilities, and talent scouting in places that have been underrepresented in the sport.

14. **Representation of Multiple Societies and Cultures:**
The rich fabric of India's cultural variety is reflected in the sport of cricket. Cricket is able to highlight the cultural diversity of the nation in a number of

different ways, including the provision of a wide variety of cuisine at stadiums and the incorporation of regional customs and musical styles into broadcasts of the game. This helps to make cricket more approachable and relatable to supporters from all over the country.

15. **Obstacles to the Cohesion of the Region:**

Cricket may help to bring people together throughout an area, but it is not without its difficulties. Grievances and conflicts are occasionally precipitated as a result of situations in which teams are selected in an unfair manner or in which players from a certain region are overrepresented overall. It is crucial for the governing bodies of cricket to retain justice and inclusivity in order to maintain the sport's function as a unifying force in the region.

The game of cricket has had a significant and long-lasting impact on the integration of India's various regions. Not only does participation in the sport offer a stage upon which to exhibit regional abilities and cultivate a sense of local pride, but it also transcends regional boundaries in order to contribute to the formation of a sense of national identity. Cricket is a unifying force that draws the entire nation of India together, despite the fact that India's language variety, cultural diversity, and geographical diversity are all sources of strength. It is a credit to the sport's significance as a binding agent in the mosaic of regional variation that it has the ability to generate feelings of enthusiasm, friendship, and a common sense of belonging in its participants. In India, cricket is more than simply a sport; it is a celebration of the country's unity despite its many cultural and religious differences.

4.1 Regional rivalries and their role in shaping cricket in India

Cricket is more than simply a sport in India; it's also a cultural phenomenon that stirs up intense feelings and a sense of identity among the country's many different regions. There is no denying the role that regional rivalries have had in the development of Indian cricket's current landscape. These rivalries, which are influenced by the country's history, geography, and culture, have been extremely important to the development of the sport across the country over the course of its history. In this essay, the historical context of regional rivalries in Indian cricket is investigated, as well as their influence on the sport, iconic rivalries, and the modern significance of these dynamics.

1. **Contextualization Historique:**

When the British first brought cricket to India during the colonial era, they were the ones responsible for planting the seeds that would later grow into fierce regional rivalries. Although the British elite dominated the early years of cricket, the Indian elite eventually took up the sport, and regional competitions started to arise about the same time. One of the earliest cricket competitions in India was called the Bombay Quadrangular, and it had teams representing

Bombay, the Hindus, the Muslims, and the Europeans. These different regional connections were reflected in the participants of the tournament.

2. **The Impact of a Regional Sense of Identity:**
The numerous linguistic, cultural, and geographical areas that make up India have always been a source of pride and individuality for the country. Cricket, despite its status as a national sport, has created a stage upon which different regions can exhibit the distinctive cricketing customs, playing styles, and abilities that are associated with them. The game has helped people from all parts of the country develop a shared appreciation for cricket while also highlighting the unique characteristics of each location.

3. **Legendary Teams from Each Region:**
The Ranji Trophy is considered to be the most prestigious domestic cricket competition in India.
It is played by regional teams that represent India's several states and regions. These teams have developed into emblems of regional pride and have been responsible for the development of some of India's most talented cricket players. The Mumbai cricket team, the Delhi cricket team, and the Karnataka cricket team, amongst others, have earned legendary status in Indian cricket due to the significant contributions they have made and the fervent support they have received from their respective fan bases.

4. **Rivalries between Different States:**
The competition between different states inside India has become an essential component of Indian cricket. Matches between regional teams, such as Mumbai versus Delhi, Karnataka versus Tamil Nadu, and Bengal versus Punjab, are eagerly anticipated and watched with zeal. These competitions foster a sense of teamwork and healthy competitiveness, which in turn contributes to the cohesion of the region and a common passion for the game.

5. **Heroes and Legends of the Community:**
Every area has had its share of cricketing greats, people who are lauded not just for their achievements on the field but also for their contributions to the development of a sense of regional pride. Players like as Sachin Tendulkar, who hails from Mumbai, Rahul Dravid, who hails from Karnataka, and Sourav Ganguly, who hails from Bengal, are not only idols of the sport of cricket but also emblems of regional identity. Their achievements have strengthened the cricketing traditions of their respective regions and established enduring legacies.

6. **Influence on the State of National Consciousness:**
Even though regional rivalries are strongly rooted in Indian cricket, the successes of the Indian cricket team on the international arena have the capacity to unite the entire nation regardless of regional boundaries. When India won the 1983 Cricket World Cup, the 2007 ICC World Twenty20, and the 2011 Cricket

World Cup, it was one of those unforgettable occasions that created a sense of national pride and solidarity that transcended regional connections.

7. **The season of the Indian Premier League (IPL):**

   The Indian Premier League (IPL), a Twenty20 cricket spectacular, is a great example of how regional identities can coexist with national unity. In this league, city-based franchises representing different parts of India compete against one another. These franchises have each created their own distinct fan bases and cultures, which serves to highlight the multifaceted nature of the nation while also making a contribution to a common Indian sense of identity.

8. **The Part Played by the Media:**

   Through the sport of cricket, India's many distinct regions are brought closer together through the power of the media, particularly television and other digital channels. Fans from every nook and cranny of the country are certain to be able to feel a connection to the game and their preferred players because to the broad coverage of the sport and the regional language commentary and analysis that is provided.

9. **Festivals and Celebrations Revolving Around Cricket:**

   In India, festivals are sometimes held to celebrate various sporting events, particularly cricket matches featuring the Indian national team. The boundaries of regions are ignored as people from all across the country congregate in one place to watch and cheer on the squad. These festivities encourage a sense of togetherness as well as a collective excitement for the sport.

10. **Effects on the Economies of the Local Area:**

    Not only have regional rivalries had an impact on the cultural and emotional fabric of Indian cricket, but they have also had a substantial impact on the sport's economic landscape. The rising popularity of the sport has stimulated the expansion of several businesses that are closely associated with it, including the media, hospitality, merchandise, and tourism. These developments have helped to contribute to the economic prosperity of areas that host cricket matches and tournaments.

11. **Obstacles to the Existence of Regional Unity:**

Regional competitions have contributed to the growth of cricket in India, although they are not without their difficulties. Grievances and conflicts are occasionally precipitated as a result of situations in which teams are selected in an unfair manner or in which players from a certain region are overrepresented overall. It is crucial for the governing bodies of cricket to retain justice and inclusivity in order to maintain the sport's function as a unifying force in the region.

Iconic regional rivalries include the following:

1. **Mumbai in contrast to Delhi:**
   The rivalry between Mumbai and Delhi is one of the longest-standing and most heated in all of Indian cricket. Cricket has a long and illustrious history in the city of Mumbai, which has given rise to a plethora of legends in the game. Delhi, the nation's capital, also has a historic cricketing background. The games that these two teams play against one another are always highly anticipated and involve a fierce level of rivalry.
2. **A matchup between Karnataka and Tamil Nadu:**
   Both Karnataka and Tamil Nadu are located in the southern region of India, and their cricketing programs are considered to be among the best in the country. Both teams have a long history and have been responsible for the development of some of the best cricket players in the country. Competition between these two states is fierce, and games between them consistently bring boisterous crowds.
3. **The Battle of Bengal and Punjab:**
   The rivalry between Bengal and Punjab exemplifies the multifaceted nature of India. The culturally diverse and historically significant state of Bengal squares off against Punjab, which is well-known for its vibrant cricketing tradition and significant accomplishments. The rivalry between these two teams often brings out the passion and pride of the local fans.
4. **The state of Karnataka takes on Andhra Pradesh.**

The conflict between the adjacent states of Karnataka and Andhra Pradesh in South India is considered to be of regional significance. These matches are closely watched by fans from both regions, and when Karnataka and Andhra Pradesh players compete against one another, they frequently find themselves in high-pressure circumstances. Fans from both regions closely follow these matches.

XIII. Significance in the Present Day:

Even in the contemporary era of Indian cricket, rivalry between different regions remain an important force. These rivalries have been exacerbated by the Indian Premier League (IPL), which pits city-based franchises with regional ties against one another in a competition for supremacy. The fervent support shown by fans for the teams in their own domestic IPL tournament contributes to a cricketing environment that is lively, competitive, and entertaining.

XIV. The Participation of Social Media:

The use of social media has been extremely important in both the escalation of regional rivalries and the engagement of fans. followers have a forum to demonstrate their allegiance to their favorite teams on social media platforms such as Twitter and Instagram, where they may also engage in pleasant banter with followers of other clubs.

XV. The Expanding Scope of Home Tournaments:

Domestic competitions such as the Ranji Trophy and the Duleep Trophy have developed throughout the years in order to maintain their prominence and level of intensity. Regional clubs are continuing to put money into the cultivation of new talent, infrastructure, and coaching in order to keep their edge over other teams.

In Indian cricket, regional rivalries are an essential component of the sport's overall structure. They not only foster a common passion for the game and a sense of national pride, but they also pay tribute to India's vast cultural variety and the unique characteristics of each of the country's regions. Indian cricket has evolved into a sport that brings the entire country closer together while also honoring the distinctive qualities and accomplishments of its various regions as a result of its rich history, culture, and the intense competitive spirit that surrounds its regional rivalries. In such a large and varied country, cricket serves as the binding agent that brings together the myriad of cultural motifs into a vivid tapestry of national cohesion and identification.

4.2 Stories of cricket promoting unity among diverse regions

In India, cricket is more than simply a sport; it is also a cultural phenomenon that has the ability to bridge geographical, linguistic, and cultural differences. In other words, cricket is India. It acts as a force that brings together different parts of the country and helps to build a sense of national identity. This essay discusses stories of cricket encouraging unity across India's varied regions, highlighting historical milestones, legendary rivalries, and unforgettable matches that have transcended regional boundaries and unified the nation. Cricket has been a unifying force for India since its inception, and this essay explores how these stories have been told.

1. **Important Occurrences in History:**
1. **The Connection Between the Independence of India and Cricket:**
   During India's fight for independence from British rule, the sport of cricket was an important factor. The potential of the sport to bring people together and further the concept of a unified India was recognized by prominent political figures such as Mahatma Gandhi. In a well-known episode, Gandhi went to see a cricket match that was being played between Hindu and Muslim teams. There, he stressed the significance of harmony among different communities.
2. **The victory in the 1983 Cricket World Cup:**
   India's triumph in the 1983 Cricket World Cup marked a watershed moment in the country's long and illustrious cricket history. The victory of the underdog team captained by Kapil Dev over the more favorably favored West Indies in the championship game sparked the interest of the entire nation. Indians of all regions, languages, and cultural backgrounds came together to celebrate their nation's success on the international arena after it was announced that India had won a historic competition.

II. Iconic Rivalries:

3. **The Rivalry Between Mumbai and Delhi:**
   One of the most heated and historically significant rivalries in domestic cricket is played out between Mumbai and Delhi. Not only do matches between these two cricketing powerhouses highlight the competition between them, but they also bring together supporters from all around the country. The fierce battle sheds light on the myriad ways in which the two areas have historically played the game of cricket.

4. **The Rivalry Between Karnataka and Tamil Nadu:**
   The rich cricketing tradition of South India is reflected in the competitive nature of the domestic cricket matchups between Karnataka and Tamil Nadu. Fans from a variety of linguistic and cultural backgrounds come together to cheer on their teams during contests between these two countries, which bring out their fiercest followers.

III. Examples of Regional Representation in Literature:

5. **The Coming of Age of Virat Kohli:**
   Virat Kohli, one of the most famous cricketers in India, plays for the Delhi area and has supporters all around the country.
   Millions of people have been motivated by his story, which began in Delhi and ended with him leading the Indian cricket team, and people from all around the country have come together to show their support for his incredible career.

6. **The Relationship to the State of Karnataka:**
   Karnataka has long been known as a breeding ground for exceptional cricket players, creating superstars such as Rahul Dravid and Anil Kumble along the way. These cricket players have risen above their regional associations to become national icons, and as a result, they have followers from all throughout India.

IV. The impact of the Indian Premier League (IPL) on the sport:

7. **The Indian Premier League: A Reflection of Unity:**
   The Indian Premier League (IPL) is a shining example of how the sport of cricket can bring together people from all over the world. In this league, city-based franchises representing different parts of India compete against one another. It has created a fan base that spans beyond the region in which a club is headquartered, as individuals from all regions of the country support for their favorite IPL franchises. The Indian Premier League (IPL) began in 2008 and is now played in India. The Indian Premier League has given fans of cricket a shared feeling of who they are as a community.

V. The Strength that Comes from Celebrating Together:

8. **Holidays Observed Nationwide:**
   Celebrations of cricket in India frequently become national events, exceeding the limits of
   individual regions. Iconic moments, such as a player scoring a century, a thrilling last-over finish, or a major victory, are celebrated with fervor across the

nation, regardless of regional ties or affiliations with specific teams. During these moments, the collective joy and unity that cricket fosters can be felt throughout the stadium.

VI. The Function of the Media

9. **A Commentary on the Regional Language:**

The broadcasting of cricket in India is not restricted to either the English language or the Hindi language alone. Fans that come from a variety of linguistic backgrounds are able to engage with the sport thanks to a major element that provides commentary in their native language.

It gives players the opportunity to experience the game in their own language, which helps forward the cause of unity and inclusivity.

10. **Comprehensive Protection:**

Because cricket receives such extensive media coverage, fans in every part of the world are able to watch matches and consume content that is relevant to cricket. Through the use of mediums such as television, radio, and digital platforms, cricket is broadcast all throughout the country, helping to create a sense of communal participation in the sport.

VII. Initiatives at the Local Level:

11. **Cricket Training and Education Programs:**

Cricket associations and organizations have begun grass-roots development programs with the intention of fostering talent from all around India. Young cricket players from all over the world, regardless of where they come from, are given the chance to participate in these programs and show off their talents.

12. **Academies for the Sport of Cricket:**

Cricket academies may be found all around the country and play an important role in the development of burgeoning cricket players. These academies embrace talents from a variety of regions, ensuring that the development of the sport is not limited to a select few locales but rather encompasses all of the world.

VIII. Festivities Celebrated in Cultures:

13. **The Integration of Cultures:**

The cultural diversity of India is frequently celebrated in many events in India, including cricket matches. The music, dances, and customs of a place often permeate the atmosphere of stadiums. Not only do these cultural manifestations make the experience of playing cricket more enjoyable, but they also help bring people together by highlighting the multicultural nature of the nation.

IX. The Language Shared by All Cricket Fans:

Cricket functions as a universal language that is able to communicate across geographical, linguistic, and cultural divides. People from different parts of the world are able to interact with one another and make friendships thanks to the sport of cricket, which helps to bring people together through a common interest.

X. Consideration of All Candidates When Forming Teams:

14. **Representation from a variety of geographical areas:**
The selection process for the Indian cricket team has gotten more open-minded over the course of its history. The national team has included players that come from a variety of locations, have come from a variety of backgrounds, and speak a variety of languages. This reflects the diversity that exists throughout India.

XI. Culture of Fans That Welcomes Everyone:

15. **Participation from a Wide Variety of Fans:**

People from different parts of India are welcome to participate in India's expansive fan culture. Fans communicate with one another and participate in conversations, transcending regional barriers while celebrating the same sport together. This can happen either in the stadium or on social media.

XII. Obstacles to Overcome and Opportunities to Seize:

Cricket has the ability to bring together many different locations, but it also has some obstacles to overcome. Instances of biased team selection, biases based on area, and opportunities that are not equally available can be barriers to the sport's inclusiveness. On the other hand, these difficulties present an opportunity for the cricket authority to create a level playing field for all of the regions.

Cricket in India has an incredible capacity to bring together people from different parts of the country and develop a common sense of national identity. The sport has repeatedly shown that it is not limited by national boundaries, linguistic barriers, or cultural norms by virtue of historical moments, rivalries that have become iconic, and accounts of regional representation. The Indian Premier League, considerable media coverage, grassroots activities, and cultural celebrations all contribute to furthering the cause of fan unity among supporters hailing from a variety of geographical areas. The power of cricket resides in its capacity to unite people from different parts of the country in a shared appreciation of the sport. This helps us to remember that, within the context of cricket, we are all members of the same team - the Indian cricket team.

4.3 The significance of the Indian Premier League (IPL) in fostering regional pride

With its one-of-a-kind combination of sporting competition and cultural celebration, the Indian Premier League (IPL) has quickly become one of the most important and influential cricket events on a global scale. In addition to its financial success and influence on cricket's development as a sport, the Indian Premier League (IPL) also plays an important part in promoting regional pride in India. Fans now have a sense of belonging and identification thanks to the Indian Premier League teams, which each represent a different area or city located somewhere in the country. In this essay, we will investigate the significance of the Indian Premier League (IPL) in encouraging regional pride as well as the causes that have contributed to the occurrence of this phenomena.

1. **Introductory Remarks:**
   The Board of Control for Cricket in India (BCCI) initiated the Indian Premier League, also known as the IPL, in the year 2008. The IPL is a common abbreviation for the Indian Premier League. The tournament pioneered a business concept centered on franchises, in which individual teams are owned by corporate entities, celebrities, and businesspeople respectively. Each team is comprised of players from a distinct Indian city or area. The Indian Premier League (IPL) brought together high-caliber cricketing action and entertainment to create a spectacle that captivates a wide range of fans who are enthusiastic about the game. As a result, the game has been transformed.

2. **Representation in the Regional Area:**
   The fact that the IPL's franchises come from different parts of the world is one of the essential features that sets it apart from other leagues. The teams represent the cultural and regional uniqueness of their respective regions, and they are named after cities or states. The Indian Premier League (IPL) is a platform that allows fans to connect with their roots and proudly support the teams from their respective regions.

3. **Iconic Franchises and the Significance They Have for Their Regions:**

1. **The Mumbai Indians:**
   One of the most successful teams in the history of the Indian Premier League is the Mumbai Indians franchise, which represents the city of Mumbai. Not only is Mumbai the financial hub of India, but it is also the center of the cricketing world in India. The city has a long history of success in cricket, producing legends such as Sachin Tendulkar along the way. Due to the fact that the Mumbai Indians represent everything that is great about Mumbai and the state of Maharashtra, they have a sizable following that goes well beyond the city limits.

2. **The Chennai Super Kings :**
   The Chennai Super Kings, which are currently managed by Mahendra Singh Dhoni, encapsulate the ethos of both the city of Chennai and the state of Tamil Nadu as a whole. The franchise enjoys a steady history of financial success and a dedicated following of customers. Cricket plays a significant role in Chennai's history and culture, and the city has a strong attachment to the sport.

3. **The Kolkata Knight Riders:**
   The franchise known as the Kolkata Knight Riders is meant to be a representation of both the
   city of Kolkata and the state of West Bengal. Bollywood actor Shah Rukh Khan is a co-owner of the team, which has garnered significant support not just in Kolkata but also in Bengali communities located throughout India and the rest

of the world. The business venture highlights the region's extensive cultural and historical background and history.

4. **The Royal Families of Rajasthan**

   The underdog mentality is something that has become synonymous with the Rajasthan Royals, who come from the state of Rajasthan. The group successfully captures the spirit of the state's regal heritage as well as its many cultural traditions. The franchise has been extremely helpful in expanding the popularity of cricket throughout the area.

5. **Royal Challengers Bangalore:**

   The Royal Challengers Bangalore franchise is considered to be the official representative of both the city of Bangalore and the state of Karnataka. The squad is well-known for the aggressive manner in which it plays, and its fan base is extremely devoted. The city of Bangalore is known as the "Silicon Valley of India," which is a reflection of the dynamic nature of the surrounding area. Bangalore is a melting pot of cultures.

6. **Sunrisers Hyderabad is the sixth team.**

   A relatively recent addition to the Indian Premier League, the Sunrisers Hyderabad franchise calls the city of Hyderabad, Telangana, home. The squad has had a lot of success and has become quite popular in a short amount of time; they are a great representation of the thriving culture and history of the area.

7. **Kings XI Punjab:**

   A deep and meaningful relationship exists between the thriving Punjabi culture and the Kings XI Punjab franchise, which represents the state of Punjab. The matches played by the team are famous for the exciting atmosphere and boisterous celebrations that they create, which are said to embody the spirit of Punjab.

8. **The Capitals of Delhi:**

The spirit that permeates India's national capital can be felt throughout the Delhi Capitals franchise. Fans from Delhi and the regions that surround it connect with the squad due to the fact that it features a mixture of local and international players.

IV. Iconic Figures in the Region:

There are local and international cricketers on each IPL franchise, but the presence of regional stars and legends is especially essential. Not only do these players represent their respective regions, but they also act as models for younger players hoping to play cricket in the same locations. The existence of hometown legends contributes to the sense of regional pride that is linked with the franchises.

V. Joyous Occasions Experienced Together:

Cities and regions across the country come to life with communal celebrations during the Indian Premier League season. The matches that include the local franchise become a focal point for fans to congregate at, watch together, and root for as a group.

During Indian Premier League matches, there is a strong feeling of community and coming together that helps build a sense of regional pride.

VI. The Effect on the Economies of the Area:

The Indian Premier League has a significant influence on the local economies of the areas that host its matches. It encourages tourists to visit the area, which in turn helps local companies and brings in money for the hospitality and entertainment industries. The economic benefits are not limited to the cities that are hosting the event but instead extend across the entire region.

VII. Participation from Fans and Competitiveness:

The matches of the Indian Premier League are more than just a game of cricket; they are also a display of the passion and pride of the various regions. The undying allegiance and fervent enthusiasm that fans demonstrate toward their home-town sports teams is clear. Fans from different regions engage in friendly banter and competition while rooting for their respective franchises, which contributes to the drama and excitement of the event.

VIII. Integration of Cultural Aspects:

The Indian Premier League incorporates several aspects of local culture into its games and other events across the country. The vast cultural diversity of India is celebrated in the stadiums through the performance of regional music, dances, and traditions. Fans get a one-of-a-kind experience as a result of the blending of culture, which also helps cultivate an appreciation of the pluralistic nature of the nation.

IX. Platforms of Digital Technology and Social Media:

The impact that the Indian Premier League has had on regional pride has been exacerbated because to the visibility of the IPL on social media and other digital channels. Fans from all across the country and even from all over the world are able to actively engage with the local franchises in their areas and convey their pride in their regions online. Fans now have a powerful new weapon at their disposal to communicate their enthusiasm and make connections with people who are motivated by the same things they are.

X. The Function of the Team Owners:

The individuals who own franchises in the Indian Premier League (IPL), many of whom are well-known figures from the surrounding area or the entertainment industry, help to foster a sense of regional pride. Because of their active participation and unbridled enthusiasm for their teams, a direct connection is established between the club and its fans.

XI. Development at the Grassroots:

Young cricketers from all over the world have been motivated to take the sport more seriously as a result of the Indian Premier League. The success of local players on IPL teams acts as inspiration for young players who aspire to play for those teams. Young cricket players are given opportunities through scouting programs and franchise academies, which contributes to the overall development of the sport at the grassroots level.

XII. Obstacles to Overcome and Opportunities to Seize:

The Indian Premier League (IPL) has had some success in boosting regional pride, but it also confronts some difficulties. Inclusivity can be hindered by things like biased squad selection, geographical prejudices, and discrepancies in the chances available to players from different locations. On the other hand, these difficulties present opportunity for the cricket authorities to ensure that all regions have a level playing field.

Fans from all over India feel a stronger sense of identification and belonging because to the success of the Indian Premier League (IPL), which has evolved into a representation of regional pride. The Indian Premier League fosters a sense of community and pride among its fans by bringing together a variety of elements, such as legendary franchises, local heroes, joint celebrations, and cultural elements. The league's economic impact, the engagement of fans, and the role that digital platforms have played have further increased its significance in the process of cultivating regional pride. The Indian Premier League (IPL) is more than simply a cricket competition; it is also a celebration of the diversity, culture, and regional identities that characterize India. As a result, it is one of the most treasured and uniting features of the sporting landscape in India.

Chapter 5

Cricket and Education

Cricket is more than simply a sport; in many countries, including India, Pakistan, England, Australia, and many more, it is even revered in the same manner as a religion. It's not only a cultural phenomena, but also a way of life, and it serves as motivation for millions of people. It has the potential to overcome barriers and bring people together, thereby promoting a sense of solidarity and pride in the community. In addition to its function as a form of entertainment, cricket has played an important part in the advancement of education and individual growth. This essay investigates the complex nature of the connection between cricket and education by looking into the history of the sport's association with education, as well as its function in fostering the development of life skills and its influence on the availability of education for disadvantaged groups.

1. **Introductory Remarks:**
   Cricket and education have a mutually beneficial relationship in which each contributes to the growth and development of the other. Cricket, as a sport, has provided a number of people with the inspiration and drive they need to pursue education and further their own personal development. On the other hand, education provides people with the information and abilities that strengthen their cricketing ability and contribute to their success in the sport. This dual impact has had a tremendous influence on the lives of many young people who are interested in pursuing a career in cricket.
2. **The historical context at this time:**
   There is a significant amount of history surrounding the relationship between cricket and education. The Marylebone Cricket Club (also known as the MCC), which was founded in London in 1787, is credited with being the first organization to formally play cricket as a sport. The Marylebone Cricket Club has strong ties to the establishment of the illustrious Lord's Cricket Ground and was affiliated with a number of notable educational institutions. Because of

the MCC's dedication to cricket as a sport, a platform was established on which educational institutions could play a significant part in directing the evolution of the game.

3. **Educational Organizations and the Sport of Cricket:**

The progression of cricket was greatly aided by the involvement of educational institutions. They have made it possible for students to pursue their interest in the sport by providing the necessary infrastructure as well as coaching. Historically, educational institutions like schools and universities have served as cradles for talent, fostering the development of aspiring cricket players while also providing them with a well-rounded educational background.

1. **The Game of Cricket at School**

   Schools, particularly in countries that are passionate about cricket, have played an important role in introducing the sport to younger students. The likes of Sachin Tendulkar, Rahul Dravid, and Sir Vivian Richards are just a few of the famous cricketers who got their start playing the game in their respective schools. In addition to teaching cricketing abilities, the discipline, teamwork, and devotion that are encouraged and fostered within the context of a school cricket match are also invaluable life qualities.

2. **Cricket at the University:**

The development of cricket talent at higher levels has been significantly aided by universities and colleges across the country. Young cricketers now have more possibilities to demonstrate their skills because to the establishment of university cricket teams and inter-collegiate championships. Additionally, academic programs that are related to sports science and administration are frequently offered at universities, which is another factor that contributes to the growth of the sport.

IV. Practical Experiences and Cricket:

Cricket is more than simply a game; it teaches fundamental life skills that are extremely beneficial to one's own growth and development. These are the kinds of abilities that can be employed in a variety of contexts throughout a person's life, and they are frequently acquired in real-world settings.

1. **Obey the rules:**

   Players develop their discipline through participation in cricket. Discipline is absolutely necessary for success in the sport, and this includes everything from being on time to playing by the rules to leading a healthy lifestyle. Players gain an understanding of the significance of commitment and devotion in the process of reaching their objectives, skills that are transferable to both their academic and professional lives.

2. **Collaboration:**

Cricket is a team sport that places an emphasis on working together and communicating effectively.

Players develop the ability to collaborate with other people in order to accomplish a goal, which is a talent that is extremely applicable in a variety of academic and professional contexts.

3. **Effective Management of Time:**

Effective time management is required in order to play cricket and be successful academically. Cricket players typically have packed schedules, and it is up to them to figure out how to balance their academic responsibilities, match preparation, and practice. This ability might be helpful in balancing the commitments that come with academic work.

4. **Coping with the Pressure:**

The sport of cricket puts its players in high-pressure circumstances, especially when the stakes are high in a contest. Exams, presentations, and other aspects of life provide excellent opportunities to hone one's ability to maintain composure and perform well despite the presence of external pressures.

5. **Communication and Effective Leadership:**

Leadership and clear communication are two of the most important factors in determining a team's level of success in cricket. It is common for captains and other senior players to take on leadership responsibilities, coaching their teams and discussing the techniques they want to use. In both educational and professional settings, these skills are absolutely necessary.

6. **Capacity for Recovery:**

Cricket, just like life, is full of both highs and lows. The journey of a cricketer often includes encounters with failures, injuries, and other types of setbacks. The ability to persevere through difficult situations and emerge stronger on the other side is a trait that is useful in both the classroom and the workplace.

V. Scholarships and other educational opportunities will be discussed next.

Cricket has helped gifted individuals have access to educational opportunities by providing scholarships and other forms of financial support. Many educational institutions and cricket academies provide financial assistance in the form of scholarships to talented young cricketers. These scholarships allow the recipients to continue their studies while also improving their cricketing abilities. The availability of these scholarships has been critical in removing monetary obstacles, which can be a barrier to receiving an education of sufficient quality.

VI. Examples of Inspiring Stories:

The history of the sport of cricket is littered with examples of people who have achieved greatness by employing cricket as a vehicle to further their studies and open doors to other opportunities.

1. **The illustrious Sir Frank Worrell:**
   Sir Frank Worrell, one of the most famous West Indian cricketers of the 20th century, was able to use his success in the game as a stepping stone to a college degree. In spite of the fact that he was struggling financially, he was granted a scholarship that allowed him to attend the University of London. It was there that he honed his cricketing skills and eventually became the captain of the West Indies cricket team.

2. **Rahul Dravid**
   Education is something that Rahul Dravid, a cricketing legend and a former captain of the Indian cricket team, feels very strongly about. While simultaneously developing his career as a cricket player, Dravid also earned a degree in commerce. Because of his dedication to both schooling and cricket, he is looked up to as a role model by a large number of young cricket players.

3. **Mithali Raj:**

The captain of the Indian women's cricket team, Mithali Raj, is known for being an outspoken supporter of educational causes. During the course of her career as a cricket player, she also earned a master's degree in humanities. Young women who strive to succeed in both education and cricket might take their cue from Raj's ability to successfully juggle the two.

VII. Cricket's Contribution to International Development:

In a variety of different programs and efforts, the game of cricket has been utilized as an instrument for educational and developmental purposes.

1. **Cricket as a Force for Good:**
   Cricket has been utilized in areas that are prone to conflict as a means of promoting peace and reconciliation. People from all walks of life come together to participate in "Cricket for Peace" and other similar programs, which use cricket as a vehicle to promote harmony and cooperation. Educative components that teach essential life skills are frequently incorporated into these types of activities.

2. **The game of street cricket**

Underprivileged youngsters are given access to the sport of cricket as well as educational help through initiatives that are becoming increasingly common in many urban areas. These programs provide an alternative to activities that may not be as attractive and teach participants discipline as well as life skills.

VIII. Obstacles and Limitations:

Cricket presents a number of difficulties and roadblocks, despite the fact that it can improve people's access to education and foster the development of life skills. These difficulties can impact persons at a wide range of educational levels and levels of cricketing aspiration.

1. **Restrictions Due to Financial Means:**
   Cricket is a sport that can be quite pricey to participate in, particularly at higher levels. For many aspiring cricket players, the expense of equipment, coaching, and travel can be prohibitive. This is especially true for those who come from economically disadvantaged families.

2. **Studying versus playing cricket:**
   Finding a balance between academics and cricket might be difficult. There is typically very little time left over for educational endeavors due to the demanding schedules of professional cricket. Young cricketers may find themselves in the difficult position of having to choose between their ardor for the game and their dedication to their schooling.

3. **Inequalities between the sexes:**

The gender imbalances in cricket are often a reflection of the gender imbalances in schooling. Because of social and cultural conventions, it may be difficult for women and girls to participate in cricket or take advantage of educational opportunities. There has been great advancement made thanks to efforts taken to promote women's cricket and education, but there are still many obstacles to overcome.

IX. Projects and Possible Solutions:

Efforts are being undertaken to address the issues that are linked with cricket and education. A variety of initiatives and solutions are being developed with the goal of establishing possibilities for aspiring cricket players while also assuring access to quality education.

1. **Fellowships and financial aid**
   Talented cricket players might receive financial assistance in the form of scholarships and awards from cricket governing bodies, educational institutions, and charitable organizations. These monetary incentives have the potential to make the burden of school costs more manageable.

2. **Programs for People with Two Careers:**
   There are dual career programs available at some colleges and cricket academies. These programs are designed to meet the academic and cricketing needs of individuals. Students are better able to maintain a healthy balance between their academic and cricketing activities with the assistance of these programs.

3. **Engagement with the Community:**
   Underprivileged youngsters are the focus of community outreach projects that provide them with opportunities to participate in cricket and receive an education. Children who would not otherwise have access to such resources as equipment, coaching, and educational support are given it through these programs.

4. **Initiatives to Promote Women's Cricket:**
   The advancement of women's cricket as well as educational opportunities is

gathering steam. Opportunities for young girls to follow their aspirations in the realms of both athletics and education are being created as a result of increased prominence and investment in women's cricket.

5. **Development at the Grassroots Level:**

Cricket governing bodies are placing more emphasis on grassroots development initiatives in an effort to discover and cultivate potential at a younger age. The goal of these programs is to cultivate a pool of talented cricket players who are able to pursue their academic goals while still pursuing their cricketing ambitions.

Cricket and education have a special and powerful connection that enables individuals to follow their hopes and ambitions in life. The game of cricket not only helps players acquire valuable life skills such as discipline, teamwork, and resiliency, but it also helps players gain access to higher education by providing scholarships and other forms of financial support. Aspiring cricket players can find a glimmer of hope in hearing the motivating tales of people who have used their success in cricket as a stepping stone to further their studies. In order to guarantee that educational pursuits and cricket may live in an amicable manner, several initiatives and organizations are hard at work to find solutions to problems and open doors of opportunity for young people. Cricket and education do not compete with one another but rather complement one another, providing individuals with an all-encompassing route to personal development and achievement. Education and the sport of cricket are a potent combination, which is why they are at the center of this cooperation.

5.1 The link between cricket and education in India

Both education and cricket are extremely influential in India, and the link between the two is one that is singular and intricate, extending far beyond the confines of the playing field and the classroom. Cricket is more than simply a sport in India; it is also a way of life, a culture, and a love for many people. Education is the most important factor in both an individual's and a society's ability to make development. This essay investigates the complex relationship between cricket and education in India, exploring the ways in which the two fields interact, have an effect on one another, and contribute to the overall growth of both individuals and the nation.

1. **Introductory Remarks:**
   Throughout the history of India, cricket and education have coexisted alongside one another and affected one another. Young people have frequently cited cricket as their primary source of motivation and drive, which has pushed them to attain excellence not only in cricket but also in their academic pursuits. Cricket and education are two components of Indian culture that cannot be separated due to the profoundly intertwined nature of their relationship inside the social fabric of the nation.

2. **The Game of Cricket as a Source of Motivation for Education:**

1. **Figures to Look Up to:**
   The sport of cricket in India has given birth to a large number of legendary players who now serve as examples for younger players who aspire to play the game. Legends such as Sachin Tendulkar, Rahul Dravid, and Virat Kohli are role models for young people not only because of their skills as cricket players but also because of their commitment to their academic pursuits. These players, who frequently thrive in their academic careers in addition to their careers as cricket players, emphasize the significance of education and encourage a large number of young people to follow in their footsteps.

2. **Athletes who are also students:**
   In India, the phrase "scholar-athlete" is frequently used to refer to cricket players who achieve a high level of success in both their athletic and intellectual endeavors. This principle is exemplified by professional cricket players such as Anil Kumble, who has a degree in engineering, and Ajinkya Rahane, who has a degree in business. These individuals demonstrate that education and cricket can live in a peaceful manner, highlighting the need of striking a balance between the two.

3. **Obtaining an Education While Engaging in Play:**

Even when they begin their careers as cricket players, a significant number of the sport's
younger players still prioritize their academic endeavors. They are able to finish their formal educations thanks to the help of flexible study schedules, remote education, and educational institutions that recognize their needs. At the same time, they are working on improving their cricketing talents. This dual achievement is only attainable as a result of the hard work and dedication of these individuals, who are committed to succeeding in both their academic and athletic endeavors.

III. Educational Organizations and the Sport of Cricket:

1. **The Game of Cricket at School**
   In India, students' early experiences in school are frequently their first exposure to the sport of cricket. Students are introduced to the sport of cricket and given the opportunity to explore their potential within the context of an organized educational setting. A significant number of well-known cricketers got their starts playing the game at the school level, like Rohit Sharma and Shikhar Dhawan, for example.

2. **Cricket at the University:**

While students are pursuing their academic degrees in universities and colleges, they have the possibility to participate in cricket competitions at higher levels. Cricket events at the collegiate level give young players the opportunity to display their skills in front of a live audience. These educational establishments also provide academic programs in fields such as sports science, coaching, and sports management, all of which contribute to the expansion of the sport.

IV. Scholarships and other forms of financial assistance

Because of the numerous cricket governing bodies, educational institutions, and charitable organizations that offer scholarships and other forms of financial assistance, the sport of cricket has become a gateway for many exceptionally bright people to obtain an education. These programs help remove some of the financial hurdles that stand in the way of students receiving a good education. Young cricketers can frequently get educational scholarships if they demonstrate a high level of talent, commitment, and potential in the game.

V. The Importance of Education to the Future Growth of Cricket:

Education is not limited to the classroom and has a significant impact on the development of cricket players. On the cricket field, having a good education and the academic knowledge and life skills it may provide can be quite beneficial. Discipline, critical thinking, teamwork, communication, and the ability to solve problems are all included in these skills.

1. **Obey the rules:**
   An individual's level of education determines their level of discipline, as it teaches them the significance of maintaining a disciplined routine, completing deadlines, and adhering to a code of conduct. It is equally important to maintain discipline on the field because this affects a player's capacity to concentrate, remain focused, and perform well under pressure.

2. **Analyzing and Judging Critically:**
   Through the cultivation of analytical and critical thinking abilities, education enables individuals to make decisions based on the best available information. Critical thinking is a very useful skill for cricket players to have on the field because they frequently need to assess various scenarios, plans, and opponents.

3. **Collaboration:**
   The value of working together is emphasized strongly in both schooling and cricket. Individuals are required to collaborate successfully with one another in order to achieve group objectives in academic projects and cricket matches. The skills of collaboration that are developed in one field can be easily transferred to another field.

4. **Transmission of information**

Both education and cricket are dependent upon clear and concise communication. On the field, players have a responsibility to communicate their plans, strategies, and feedback in an understandable manner. This ability is valuable not just in the professional world but also in the academic world.

VI. Obstacles and Limitations:

Although the connection between education and cricket in India is quite strong, there are still many difficulties and roadblocks that stand in the way of individuals pursuing different levels of education and different levels of cricket.

1. **Restrictions Due to Financial Means:**

   Aspiring cricketers may find themselves at a disadvantage when it comes to the money side of things.

   Those who come from economically challenged situations may find it difficult to participate in cricket because the expense of coaching, equipment, and travel might be exorbitant. It's possible that the financial burden will prevent them from getting a good education or participating in cricket activities.

2. **Striking a Balance Between Cricket and Academics:**

   Young cricketers who aspire to play professionally often find themselves with little time for educational endeavors since their schedules are so packed. Many aspiring cricket players struggle to find a balance between their scholastic pursuits and their passion for the game. The pressure to perform in both of these areas can be overpowering, forcing some people to make choices that are challenging for them.

3. **Inequalities between the sexes:**

   Both the field of cricket and the field of education suffer from gender imbalances, which frequently mirror one another. As a result of social and cultural constraints, it is possible for women and girls to have restricted access to educational opportunities and high-quality cricket coaching. While there has been progress made in advancing women's cricket and education, there are still many obstacles to overcome.

4. **Differences Between Regions:**

There are huge regional variations in India when it comes to access to high-quality education and cricket facilities. In places where there are few chances and few resources, talented people frequently go unnoticed. Building bridges between these two groups is a constant issue.

The relationship between education and cricket in India is evidence of the transformative potential of both athletics and learning for both individuals and entire communities. Cricket has been a source of motivation for a large number of young people, encouraging them to continue their education in addition to pursuing their goals of playing cricket. In turn, education provides cricket players with necessary life skills and discipline, which improves their performance while they are competing. Education is made more accessible to young cricketers through the availability of scholarships and other forms of financial help, which break down financial obstacles. Even while difficulties still exist, the actions and solutions that are already in place are gradually paving the way for a future in which cricket and education can coexist happily, thereby offering opportunities for comprehensive growth and achievement. Cricket and education both serve as pillars of aspiration and empowerment, which shape the lives of people as well as the lives of the nation as a whole. At the core of this relationship is the fact that the two are intertwined.

5.2 Scholarship programs and cricket academies

Cricket, a sport that is played with great fervor and has a significant cultural impact, has a significant following in many nations, including India, Australia, England, and many more. The hope of playing cricket for their country on the world stage serves as a potent inspiration for young people who are interested in the sport. Nevertheless, in order to make this ambition a reality, you will often need access to high-quality coaching, facilities, and educational assistance. In this essay, we will investigate the function that cricket academies and scholarship programs have in the development of cricketing talent as well as scholastic aspirations. These programs play a critical part in discovering and cultivating young talent while simultaneously offering access to education. This enables aspiring cricket players to improve in every aspect, which is essential for the sport.

1. **Introductory Remarks:**

   In many countries, playing cricket is more than just a recreational activity; it's ingrained in the culture. A large number of promising young cricket players harbor the hope that one day they would be selected to compete for their country's team, receive praise for their performances, and rise to the highest levels of excellence in the game. These aspirations might be brought closer to fruition through the participation in cricket academies and scholarship programs. They not only give young cricketers the essential training and resources, but they also ensure that they have access to education, which enables them to pursue their academic goals in line with their cricketing ambitions.

2. **Scholarship Programs for the Development of Cricketing Talent**

The identification and development of potential in cricket is facilitated significantly by scholarship schemes. These programs provide young cricketers with financial help, mentorship, and advice. This enables the young cricketers to obtain the greatest coaching available, access facilities that are on the cutting edge of technology, and participate in competitive cricket.

1. **Availability of High-Quality Coaching:**

   The participants of scholarship programs frequently have access to qualified and expert instructors who can hone their abilities and approaches. These coaches provide young cricket players with individualized instruction, assisting them in realizing their full potential.

2. **Facilities That Are Up to Date With Technology:**
   A significant number of educational grants and awards are presented in conjunction with reputable cricket academies or instruction facilities. These facilities provide a modern infrastructure, which is necessary for polishing talents. This infrastructure includes pitches, nets, fitness centers, and technology-assisted training, among other things.

3. **Participation in Highly Competitive Cricket:**
   Scholarship winners are frequently offered the possibility to take part in competitive matches and tournaments. They are more equipped to handle the rigors of professional cricket as a result of this exposure, which helps them gain valuable experience and cultivate a competitive spirit.

4. **Mentoring and directing others:**
   Mentorship and advice are provided to up-and-coming cricket players by seasoned cricket players and coaches who are involved with various scholarship programs. They give players an understanding of the mental and psychological components of the game, which helps players get ready for the demands of playing cricket professionally.

5. **Support in the Amount of Money:**

Scholarship programs almost always include some sort of monetary support for recipients. It helps cover fees linked to coaching, equipment, travel, and participation in tournaments, alleviating young cricketers and their families of the financial burden that comes along with playing the sport.

III. Varieties of Scholarship Programs That Are Available:
Scholarship programs in the sport of cricket can take many different forms, each of which has its own distinct emphasis and eligibility requirements.

1. **Scholarships Offered by the Government:**
   As part of their efforts to encourage participation in sports, a number of nations' governments provide cricket scholarships to promising young players. It is typical for these scholarships to also pay the costs of the athletes' academic pursuits, ensuring that they are able to achieve their academic goals.

2. **Scholarships offered by the Cricket Board:**
   Scholarship programs are offered by many cricket governing bodies across the world, including the Board of Control for Cricket in India (BCCI), Cricket Australia, and the England and Wales Cricket Board (ECB). These initiatives seek to recognize and cultivate youthful potential by providing the participants with financial assistance and other educational options.

3. **Scholarships from private organizations:**

Additionally, the support of young cricketers comes from a variety of sources, including people, private groups, and foundations. The funding for these scholarships typically comes from charitable individuals who are interested in making an investment in the sport of cricket's future.

IV. Examples of Past Achievements:

A significant number of cricketers who have achieved fame got their starts in the game by participating in scholarship programs. These examples of achievement can serve as motivation for aspiring young artists.

1. **Sachin Tendulkar: the world's best batsman**

   At the age of 14, the legendary Indian cricketer Sachin Tendulkar was awarded a scholarship by the Sir Frank Worrell Foundation. He was able to pursue his passion for cricket with the assistance of the financial support granted by the scholarship.

2. **Ellyse Perry:**

Ellyse Perry, an Australian all-rounder, was recognized early in her career by the Sydney Cricket Club with a scholarship to attend the institution. She was able to maintain a healthy balance between her academic and cricketing obligations, which ultimately led to her being one of the best female cricketers in the world.

V. Obstacles and Limitations:

Scholarship programs play an important role in the development of cricketing ability, but they are not without their share of difficulties and obstructions.

1. **Very limited quantities available:**

   Scholarship programs are not accessible to all young cricketers, which results in a restricted

   pool of potential candidates. There is often a lot of rivalry for these scholarships, and unfortunately, not all talented students will be able to win one of them.

2. **Differences Between Regions:**

   The availability of different scholarship programs can be affected by factors such as location. Those who are talented but come from less fortunate locations may not have the same exposure to the game or the same possibilities as those who come from more developed cricketing cities.

3. **Long-term viability:**

It is difficult to create scholarship programs that can be maintained throughout time. They frequently rely on finance, and the possibility exists that the programs will not operate at their full potential if the financial backing is not reliable.

VI. Cricket academies, which focus on the development of cricketing talent and education:

Cricket academies are educational establishments that are committed to the growth of young cricket players. These academies provide all-encompassing training programs that cover a variety of domains, including mental and physical preparation, physical fitness, and educational support.

1. **Instruction That Is All-Encompassing:**
   Cricket academies offer comprehensive training that focuses on all aspects of the game, including batting, bowling, fielding, and overall fitness. The training is designed to improve a cricket player's performance in all aspects of the game.
2. **Experienced Mentors:**
   Academies typically hire seasoned instructors who have a comprehensive knowledge of the sport to instruct aspiring players. These coaches offer young athletes invaluable insights and direction in their development.
3. **A Look at the Video:**
   The performance and skill of players are evaluated through video analysis at many different academies. This strategy, which is helped by technology, helps discover areas that could use some work.
4. **Assistance with Educational Matters:**

Cricket academies frequently work in conjunction with other educational institutions in order to supply their trainees with academic support. Because of this support, aspiring young cricketers will be able to pursue their educational goals while also improving their cricketing abilities.

VII. The Various Forms That Cricket Academies Can Take:

Cricket academies can range in size and scope, with some concentrating on teaching younger players while others teach more advanced players.

1. **Community-Based Learning Opportunities:**
   Young children are the primary focus of grassroots academies, which teach them the fundamentals of cricket and encourage them to develop a passion for the sport.
2. **The Most Prestigious Schools:**
   Cricket players who have reached an advanced skill level and have the ability to compete at a high level are the target audience for elite academies. These academies put their students through rigorous training and are primarily concerned with preparing them for professional cricket.
3. **Women's Academies**

As a result of the expansion of women's cricket, a number of academies are now dedicated solely to the development of female talent. These academies have the mission of encouraging and assisting women who play cricket at all skill levels.

VIII. Some Examples of Our Achievements

Numerous players' careers have been significantly influenced by the cricket academies they attended when they were younger.

1. **Rahul Dravid:**
   The KSCA academy in Bangalore was where Rahul Dravid, better known by his nickname "The Wall" for his flawless batting style, acquired his instruction. In terms of his growth as a cricketer, the academy was absolutely essential to his success.

2. **Here's Steve Smith:**

Training was provided for the former captain of the Australian cricket team, Steve Smith, at the Wests-UC Cricket Club academy in Sydney. The program equipped him with the necessary abilities and gave him the support he needed to develop into a batsman of world-class caliber.

IX. Obstacles and Limiting Factors:

Cricket academies, like any other institution, confront a variety of difficulties and obstacles that must be overcome.

1. **Availability to all:**
   Because not all areas have the same level of access to cricket academies of a high standard, there are geographical differences. It may be difficult for players from less fortunate locations to gain access to these amenities.

2. **Cost:**
   Many aspiring cricket players are unable to afford the tuition at prestigious cricket academies because the expense of training there can be very high. Talented people may be dissuaded from pursuing their goals due to financial constraints.

3. **Assistance with Education:**

The educational support provided by cricket academies varies widely, despite the fact that all of them teach cricket. It is of the utmost importance to ensure that young cricketers can successfully juggle their cricketing and academic obligations.

Scholarship opportunities and training opportunities at cricket academies are two crucial foundations that support the development of prospective players. They seek for, cultivate, and cultivate talent in cricket by providing financial support, extensive instruction, and educational help. The next generation of cricket players are inspired by success stories like those of Sachin Tendulkar and Ellyse Perry, which demonstrate that these programs can convert ambitions into reality. Even if difficulties and obstructions still exist, it is vital for continued efforts to be made to improve the accessibility, sustainability, and educational support of cricket academy scholarship programs and other cricket-related organizations. In countries that are passionate about cricket, the connection between fostering cricketing talent and scholastic aspirations is a powerful force that creates a road for young talents to accomplish their goals both on and off the cricket field. In the center of this symbiotic relationship are scholarship programs and cricket academies, which serve as guiding lights for aspiring cricket players and serve as beacons of hope for those aspiring cricket players.

5.3 How cricket has influenced educational aspirations

Cricket, which is frequently described to as a religion in countries such as India, has an unquestionable influence on the lives and aspirations of millions of different people around the world. It is more than simply a game; it has the potential to change people's life and significantly affect their educational goals and aspirations. This essay investigates the ways in which cricket has impacted educational goals, diving into the function of the sport as a source of inspiration, the scholarship chances it provides, and the life skills it instills. All of these aspects add to a more well-rounded strategy for one's own development and evolution as a person.

1. **Introductory Remarks:**
   Individuals who live in countries who are passionate about cricket have a special place in their hearts for the sport. For many individuals, cricket is more than simply a game; it's a way of life. Individuals, particularly young people who are interested in playing cricket, can be uniquely motivated and influenced by the sport, which possesses a distinctive potential to do so. This effect extends beyond the confines of the cricket pitch, making its way into classrooms and influencing the educational goals of a great number of persons.
2. **The Role of Cricket as a Motivating Factor:**

Individuals have always been motivated by the game of cricket to thrive in a variety of facets of life, including education, because cricket has always been a source of inspiration. The accomplishments of cricketing greats throughout history and the thrill that comes from playing the game itself serve as a potent source of motivation.

1. **Figures to Look Up to:**
   The sport of cricket has a history of producing great people who can act as role models not only for aspiring cricketers but also for pupils. Legends such as Sachin Tendulkar, Sir Vivian Richards, and Ricky Ponting have not only been successful on the cricket field, but they have also demonstrated attributes such as devotion, perseverance, and a strong work ethic. These characteristics are equally vital in the pursuit of education.
2. **The Ambition to Achieve Excellence:**
   The relentless pursuit of perfection in cricket is illustrative of what may be accomplished through consistent effort and unwavering commitment. Aspiring

cricket players witness this endeavor and frequently apply the same concepts to their education, with the intention of achieving greatness in their studies as well.

3. **Two Stories of Unparalleled Success:**

A significant number of cricketers, particularly those hailing from nations such as India, have managed to combine their cricketing careers with successful academic endeavors. These examples of individuals who have excelled in both their athletic and intellectual pursuits demonstrate how well cricket and education can coexist.

III. Scholarships and Other Financial Aid:

Scholarship programs in cricket are extremely important because they allow talented young cricketers to receive financial assistance so that they can pursue their educational goals. These programs provide monetary aid and enable participants to gain access to educational opportunities of a high standard all while improving their cricketing abilities.

1. **Assistance in Financial Matters:**
   Scholarship opportunities are among the most significant ways in which cricket can impact educational aspirations. These scholarships often cover a student's educational expenses, which may include tuition fees, book costs, and other charges associated with their chosen field of study. They ease the financial strain, making it possible for more people to obtain an education of high quality.

2. **Availability of High-Quality Coaching:**
   A common benefit of scholarship programs is access to high-caliber coaching and facilities. Aspiring cricket players can develop their talents while continuing their schooling thanks to programs like this one. This guarantees that they are able to adequately balance both of the responsibilities.

3. **Assistance with Education:**
   Scholarships typically include some form of educational assistance for the recipient, guaranteeing that they will be able to successfully balance their scholastic responsibilities with their commitments to cricket. This help may take the form of adaptable timetables, individual or group tutoring, and direction.

4. **Examples of Our Achievements:**

Many cricket players who have been awarded scholarships have gone on to have tremendous success in both their cricket careers and their academic endeavors. These tales are meant to serve as a source of motivation for the following generation.

IV. Skills for Daily Living:

The game of cricket teaches valuable life lessons that can be applied to other areas, such as education and personal growth. Discipline, working well with others, leadership, managing one's time effectively, and resiliency are among these skills.

1. **Obey the rules:**
   Players in cricket are expected to maintain a high level of discipline by sticking to rigorous

   training schedules, diets, and daily routines. Students get an understanding of the significance of effective time management and dedication via the use of this discipline in their academic lives.

2. **Collaboration:**
   Cricket is a team sport that places an emphasis on working together and cooperating with your teammates. Young people who play cricket acquire the ability to collaborate with others to accomplish a common objective, which is a skill that is highly transferable to academic group assignments and extracurricular activities.

3. **Effective Management of Time:**
   Effective time management is required in order to play cricket and be successful academically.

   Cricket players typically have busy schedules, and they need to make sure they leave enough time to practice, play matches, and study. The ability to effectively manage one's time is absolutely necessary for academic achievement.

4. **The Role of Communication and Leadership:**
   Leadership and the ability to communicate effectively are two skills that are essential in cricket. It is common for captains and other senior players to take on leadership responsibilities, coaching their teams and discussing the techniques they want to use. These abilities are necessary in a variety of settings, including educational and professional ones.

5. **Coping with the Pressure:**
   The sport of cricket puts its players in high-pressure circumstances, especially when the stakes are high in a contest. Exams, presentations, and other forms of academic competition give unique opportunities for students to demonstrate their ability to maintain composure and perform effectively under stress.

6. **Capacity for Recovery:**

Cricket, just like life, is full of both highs and lows. The journey of a cricketer often includes encounters with failures, injuries, and other types of setbacks. The ability to persevere through difficult situations and emerge stronger on the other side is a trait that is useful in both the classroom and the workplace.

V. Striking a Balance:

The pursuit of a cricket career while also pursuing an education can be difficult, but many prospective cricket players have been able to effectively combine the two. The impact that cricket has had on their goals to further their studies may be seen in their ability to achieve a balance between the two.

1. **Education That Can Be Tailor-Made:**
   Adaptable educational programs that are tailored to the requirements of young cricketers have been developed and implemented by a number of educational institutions and cricket bodies. Because of this flexibility, students are able to fulfill their academic responsibilities while also pursuing their aspirations of playing cricket.
2. **The Supporting Structures:**

The emotional and logistical assistance that young cricketers receive from their parents, coaches, and mentors is critical to their development as players. They guide them through the difficulties of juggling the demands of both study and cricket.

VI. Equality of the Sexes:
Cricket has not just had a big impact on the educational goals of males; the impact of cricket on women's educational aspirations has also been tremendous. The expansion of women's cricket has made it easier for young girls to pursue their educational aspirations as well as their desires of playing cricket.

1. **Women Who Inspire Other Cricket Players:**
   Female cricketers who have achieved great success, like as Mithali Raj, Meg Lanning, and Ellyse Perry, have shattered stereotypes and encouraged younger females to pursue both schooling and the sport of cricket. They act as examples to follow for young women who are interested in playing cricket.
2. **Scholarship Programs Aimed Specifically toward Women**

There has been a recent uptick in the number of scholarship programs designed specifically for female cricket players, offering both financial assistance and educational opportunities. These programs are extremely helpful in fostering gender equality not only in cricket but also in the academic sphere.

Cricket is a powerful force that has the ability to improve the lives of a large number of people by encouraging them to pursue their educational goals. Cricket can be a source of inspiration, a driver for academic performance, and a teacher of life skills that are vital in terms of both education and personal growth. Scholarship programs in cricket offer young cricketers financial aid as well as access to high-quality educational opportunities, which enables them to efficiently balance both of their pursuits. The next generation is inspired to dream big and put in a lot of effort when they hear about the achievements of people who have excelled in both cricket and education. Cricket and education share a special and mutually beneficial connection that enables individuals to realize their goals both on and off the field of play. This relationship is a unique example of symbiosis. Cricket, which is at the core of this cooperation, acts as a catalyst for educational success, hence creating opportunities for opportunities for holistic growth and personal development.

Chapter 6

Cricket and Social Initiatives

One of the sports that is played and watched the most around the world is cricket, which is sometimes referred to as a "gentleman's game." Cricket has played a key role in a variety of social activities, despite the fact that it is mostly renowned for its exciting matches, iconic players, and devoted following. This essay investigates the complex relationship between the sport of cricket and various social projects, delving into the ways in which the game has been a driving force behind positive social change and progression across a variety of societal domains.

Cricket's Role in Bridging Social Gaps

Cricket has the extraordinary capacity to bridge cultural divides and unite players hailing from a wide range of origins and experiences. It functions as a unifying force that spans gaps and overcomes obstacles of geography, culture, and society. Cricket is more than simply a sport; it is also a cultural phenomenon in many nations, including England, India, and Pakistan, for example. It brings people from different groups together, helps them build relationships with one another via the common experience of participating in sports, and fosters social cohesion.

The Role of Cricket in Defining National Identity

Cricket frequently serves as a metaphor for the identity and pride of a nation. It ends up becoming a source of national togetherness as well as a purpose for the nation. When the national cricket team of a country competes in an international tournament, it is not just about the individuals on the field; rather, it is about the hopes and dreams of the country as a whole. A successful performance by a national cricket team can provide a boost to national morale and foster a sense of belonging, so contributing to an increased sense of 'oneness' among the country's inhabitants.

The game of diplomacy and cricket

Cricket has also been utilized as a diplomatic instrument in order to de-escalate tense situations and forward the cause of world peace. Iconic matches such as 'Cricket Diplomacy' between India and Pakistan in 1987 and, more recently, the revival of cricketing ties between India and Pakistan in 2022, have been considered as a tool to enhance political relations and create an environment that is suitable for communication and cooperation.

Cricket for the Purpose of Social Progress

Cricket has not only served as a unifying factor, but it has also played an important role in a number of different social activities. These programs cover a wide range of topics, including gender equality and inclusion, as well as education and health.

Cricket in the Interest of Education

Education is one of the most important pillars supporting the growth of society. In a number of countries, education has been improved through the sport of cricket, which is played there. For instance, the "Right to Play" charity incorporates cricket into its curriculum in order to pique children's interest in education while also building an appreciation for athletics. They achieve their goals of increasing school attendance and creating an environment that is favorable to learning by capitalizing on the popularity of cricket.

Cricket and Physical Condition

One further area that has benefited from cricket's positive influence is the encouragement of healthy lifestyles. Cricket tournaments are held by a number of different groups in an effort to bring attention to important health issues such as obesity, diabetes, and cardiovascular illnesses. These events encourage people to be physically active and serve as a platform for educating communities on the significance of being active on a regular basis and consuming a diet that is nutritionally balanced.

Women's Cricket and the Struggle for Gender Equality

Cricket has historically been a male-dominated sport, but in recent years women's cricket has made great gains toward gender parity in the sport. Not only is the rise of women's cricket a sign of progress toward gender equality, but it is also a driver of such equality. Women and young girls gain confidence and independence as a result of the opportunity to pursue their ambitions in a sector that has historically been controlled by men. Women's Cricket for Change and other groups have the mission of expanding the opportunities available to women in the sport of cricket and bringing them greater prominence.

Cricket for the Inclusion of People with Disabilities

Cricket has also expanded its reach in order to encourage inclusion for people with various kinds of disability. Cricket has been modified to accommodate people with a variety of limitations, including those who are deaf, physically challenged, or visually impaired. These modifications not only make it possible for people with disabilities to take part in activities, but they also remove limitations and misconceptions held by society regarding what these people are capable of accomplishing.

The Profits and Losses of Cricket and Their Social Implications

The commercial side of cricket is also involved in various community-oriented endeavors. The sport of cricket has grown into an enterprise worth several billions of dollars, with large revenue streams coming from television rights, sponsorships, merchandise, and other areas. Because of their substantial financial resources, cricket boards, teams, and players are now more aware of their obligations to the community.

Charity Work Done by Cricket Players

Several cricketers from different countries all over the world are involved in charitable activities. They make use of their notoriety and wealth in order to contribute positively to society. For instance, cricketers Sachin Tendulkar, Virat Kohli, and Shane Warne have founded foundations and charities that work toward a variety of social concerns, ranging from education to healthcare. These foundations and charities seek to help those in need.

Sponsorships that Serve a Greater Objective

The brand images of companies that sponsor cricket teams and events are increasingly being aligned with charitable and community-oriented activities. They showcase their dedication to corporate social responsibility by utilizing their affiliation with cricket as a platform. This not only improves the image of the companies, but it also contributes to a variety of other charitable and community-based efforts.

The Obstacles and the Criticisms

Cricket and social projects have a mutually beneficial relationship; nonetheless, there are obstacles and criticisms that must be overcome in order to move further.

The process of cricket's commercialization

The increasing commercialization of cricket has given rise to questions over the genuineness and purity of the sport. Some people believe that the pursuit of riches should not take precedence over the social issues that cricket may be supporting, but others disagree. Because of its increased commercialization, cricket may become more difficult to play for people of lower socioeconomic status.

The absence of uniformity

The influence that cricket has had on many social initiatives varies greatly from country to country. Cricket is a potent instrument for social change in countries like India, but it is possible that it does not have the same level of influence in other countries that play cricket. The allocation of opportunities and resources is likewise unequal, which contributes to the further widening of the gap.

Disparities Between the Sexes

There are still major gender gaps in terms of salary, recognition, and opportunity in cricket, despite the fact that women's cricket has made tremendous strides forward in recent years. It is necessary to make an effort to solve these gaps in order to make the sport have the greatest possible impact on social objectives.

Cricket and philanthropic endeavors have a mutually beneficial partnership that has the capacity to effect positive societal change. Cricket, with its enormous following and reach, have the capacity to bring people from different countries together, as well as promote education, health, gender equality, and inclusiveness, and create possibilities for individuals to make a positive effect. However, it is of the utmost importance to strike a balance between the commercial sides of the sport and its social duties, redress imbalances, and make certain that the impact of the sport is utilized for the overall improvement of society. The relevance of cricket extends far beyond the boundary ropes, and the sport has played and will continue to play an important part in the development of our planet. One indication of this significance is the role that cricket has played in various social initiatives.

6.1 Charitable work and social responsibility by cricketers

The sport of cricket, which is frequently lauded for its tense matches and legendary players, has an influence that goes well beyond the boundary. Cricket players, in their role as global ambassadors for the sport, have shown a strong commitment to philanthropic endeavors and to taking responsibility for their communities. This essay explores the crucial role that cricketers play in charity and their commitment to making a positive impact on society. Cricket is a team sport played in the United Kingdom.

The Influence of Cricket's Most Famous Players

Cricket players occupy a special niche in today's culture. Their behavior is subject to intense scrutiny because they are not only athletes but also celebrities who hold significant sway in their respective fields. Because of their famous status, they have access to a platform that enables them to bring attention to a variety of social issues, organize support for those issues, and have a positive impact. The wide variety of volunteer efforts and programs for social responsibility that cricket players participate in exemplifies the power that cricket players possess as agents of change.

Utilizing the Power That They Have

The popularity of cricketers stretches to millions of people all around the world, and they have a devoted fan following that follows them everywhere they go. They use their popularity to bring attention to important societal issues, motivate their fans to take constructive action, and urge them to get engaged in a wide variety of charitable endeavors.

Access to the Available Resources

A significant number of cricketers enjoy financial success and have ready access to a wealth of resources. Because of their secure financial situation, they are able to make considerable donations to charitable organizations and other social causes. They frequently form their own foundations and organizations in order to give back to the issues that are important to them.

Advocacy and Financial Support Collection

Cricketers engage in advocacy efforts and fundraising activities, both on their own and in conjunction with pre-existing charity organizations. Cricketers can be found participating in both of these activities in their personal capacities. Their participation frequently attracts the attention of sponsors, corporations, and the media, which ultimately contributes to the generation of large sums for a variety of different social causes.

Some Instances of the Charitable Work Done by Cricket Players

The Influence That Sachin Tendulkar Has Had on Education

The great Indian cricketer Sachin Tendulkar is also a fervent supporter of educational opportunities for children. He is known for establishing the Sachin Tendulkar Foundation, which is dedicated to assisting disadvantaged youngsters in India with access to high-quality educational opportunities. The Tendulkar Foundation is responsible for the construction of schools, the provision of scholarships, and the support of educational activities all around the nation.

The Foundation Named After Virat Kohli

The Indian cricket team is led by captain Virat Kohli, who is well-known for his commitment to a variety of charitable causes. The mission of the 'Virat Kohli Foundation' is to improve the quality of life for disadvantaged children by promoting their participation in athletics and education. In addition, the organization provides financial support for humanitarian aid and healthcare activities.

Work Done by Shane Warne Concerning Various Health Concerns

The Shane Warne Foundation" was established by the former Australian cricketer Shane Warne with the intention of enhancing the quality of life for children who are disadvantaged or chronically ill. The foundation has been successful in raising money for children's hospitals and for medical research, and it also helps disadvantaged children and their families.

The Fight Against Trafficking in Human Beings Led by Brendon McCullum

Brendon McCullum, a former captain for New Zealand, is passionate about putting a stop to the practice of human trafficking. He has collaborated closely with organizations that are committed to avoiding and treating this problem, and he has used his prominence to increase awareness of, as well as financial support for, the cause.

Beyond All Frontiers, a Responsibility to Society

Charity work is something that cricket players perform all throughout the world, not just in their own country. They frequently extend their charity activity to other regions and countries, which demonstrates that they have a global perspective on their obligation to the community.

In Times of Crisis, Efforts to Provide Relief

The sport of cricket has been quick to mobilize in the face of natural disasters and humanitarian crises. They put their power to use to bring in money and other resources to help those affected by the calamity. For instance, in the wake of the tsunami that struck the Indian Ocean in 2004, cricket players from a variety of countries banded together to organize a fundraiser for the people that had been impacted.

Initiatives for International Health

The sport of cricket has been an important contributor to the advancement of global health efforts. The game has played a significant role in the fight against infectious diseases like HIV/AIDS, malaria, and polio, among others. Cricket players frequently take part in initiatives to raise awareness for various treatment, preventative, and vaccine programs.

Activities Benefiting a Good Cause

Cricket players take part in charity matches, exhibitions, and other events all over the world rather frequently. In addition to contributing to worthy causes, the participation in these events not only helps generate money but also gives fans the opportunity to communicate directly with the athletes they admire.

The Obstacles and the Criticisms

Criticisms of Being Too Selective

Some detractors believe that cricketers frequently support causes that either coincide with their own personal interests or offer them the opportunity for positive exposure. They argue that because of this choice, the most important societal problems are not necessarily being addressed.

Lack of Openness and Communication

It has come to our attention that certain cricketers' charitable foundations have been plagued by incidents of poor management and a lack of transparency. It is crucial for cricketers to guarantee that the philanthropic activity they do complies with ethical standards and best practices in order to preserve their credibility and sustain their fans' faith.

Dependence on the Influence of Celebrities

Although the influence of cricketers can motivate huge contributions to philanthropic causes, it may also lead to a dependence on the participation of celebrities in such causes. It is essential for long-term success to foster participation from a wider segment of the community and make certain that projects may continue even after a cricketer has finished their active playing career.

Cricket players play a significant part in humanitarian activity and social responsibility by utilizing their power and resources to bring about positive change in the world. They go above and beyond the call of duty required of them as athletes by taking on the obligations of global ambassadors and champions for a variety of social concerns. In spite of obstacles and criticisms, it is impossible to deny the impact that cricketers have had on charity, and their dedication to making the world a better place continues to serve as a source of motivation for many. Beyond the boundary, cricket players will continue to serve as a source of inspiration and a catalyst for change so long as they continue to use their platform for the betterment of society.

6.2 Cricket as a platform for addressing social issues

Cricket, which is frequently referred to as a game for gentlemen, has developed throughout the years into something that is more than just a sport. Beyond its traditional function as a source of amusement, it has transformed into a potent forum for discussing and bringing attention to a wide range of pressing societal concerns. This essay investigates the significant impact that cricket has had as a forum for discussing social concerns, bringing light on the many different ways in which the sport has been used to promote positive change in society. Specifically, this investigation focuses on the role that cricket has played in the Indian Cricket Association (ICA).

The Importance of Cricket in Contemporary Society

Since its inception, the sport of cricket has won the affection of many people all over the world. It's not just a game; it's a cultural phenomena and a feeling that people of all different nationalities, ethnicities, and religions may share in common. Because of its widespread reach and widespread popularity, the sport is a perfect vehicle for tackling a variety of social issues, including health and education, gender equality and inclusion, and more.

Fostering Cohesion and a Sense of National Pride

Cricket is a sport that brings people together, particularly in nations where the game is both a popular pastime and an integral part of the national identity. When the national cricket team of a country enters the field to play a match, they are not simply a set of players competing in a sport; rather, they are a symbol of the ambitions and dreams of that country. The accomplishments of the national team have the potential to improve national morale, develop a sense of pride, and foster a sense of belonging among the country's population.

Promoting International Relations and Peace

Cricket has also been utilized as a diplomatic instrument to defuse tense political situations and advance the cause of world peace on multiple occasions. It has been suggested that iconic matches, such as "Cricket Diplomacy" between India and Pakistan in 1987, as well as the return of cricketing links between these two nations in 2022, can serve as a tool to improve political relations and create an environment that is amenable to communication and cooperation.

Bringing Attention to Social Problems

The worldwide reach of cricket and the attention it attracts present a one-of-a-kind opportunity to bring attention to important social issues. The sport, which is frequently and widely covered by the media, has the ability to shed light on current issues, thereby raising awareness and mobilizing resources for the purpose of finding solutions to those issues. Players and tournaments in the sport of cricket have the potential to serve as advocates and spokespersons for a variety of social concerns.

The Role of Cricket as a Change Agent

Donations and Fundraising for Charitable Organizations

Cricket matches, particularly high-profile ones such as World Cups and bilateral series, are good possibilities for charitable groups to raise money through fundraising. Cricket associations frequently collaborate with non-governmental organizations (NGOs) to generate money for a variety of causes, including healthcare, education, and disaster relief. For instance, the "Cricket for Good" campaign, which is run in conjunction between the Australian Cricket Association (ACA) and UNICEF, helps generate money to promote the education and health of children all over the world.

Fostering Good Health and Physical Fitness

The sport of cricket is quite taxing on the body and needs its participants to keep up a high degree of physical fitness. People are inspired to lead more active lifestyles as a result of the emphasis placed on health and fitness.

Cricketers frequently take part in initiatives and programs designed to encourage fans and members of the general public to lead physically active and nutritionally sound lifestyles.

Putting an Emphasis on Education

A significant number of cricket organizations and players are committed to providing active support for educational projects. 'Right to Play' and other organizations use the popularity of cricket as a way to get kids interested in learning while also encouraging a passion for sports. They want to increase school attendance and foster a climate that is beneficial to learning, and they are using cricket as the vehicle to do it.

Enhancing Women's Agency

The increasing participation of women in cricket is not just an indication of progress toward gender parity but also a driver of innovation. Women and young girls gain confidence and independence as a result of the opportunity to pursue their ambitions in a sector that has historically been controlled by men. Women's Cricket for Change and other groups have the mission of expanding the opportunities available to women in the sport of cricket and bringing them greater prominence.

Fostering Acceptance And Inclusion

Cricket has also expanded its reach in order to encourage inclusion for people with various kinds of disability. Cricket has been modified to accommodate people with a variety of limitations, including those who are deaf, physically challenged, or visually impaired. These modifications not only make it possible for people with disabilities to take part in activities, but they also remove limitations and misconceptions held by society regarding what these people are capable of accomplishing.

Notable Instances Where Cricket Has Addressed Various Social Problems

Laureus Foundation for Sport in the Service of Humanity

The Laureus Sport for Good Foundation uses the power of cricket and other sports to improve the lives of children and young people who come from disadvantaged backgrounds. The foundation provides financial assistance and other forms of support to programs that employ the sport of cricket as a vehicle for inculcating morals, delivering instruction, and encouraging participants to make constructive life decisions.

Charity Competitions and Other Events

Cricket players frequently take part in charity matches and other events in order to raise money for a variety of important humanitarian causes.

These matches generate a substantial amount of revenue since they attract the attention of spectators, the media, and corporate sponsors. One such event is the "Cricket for Heroes" charity match held in England, which donates the proceeds to various military-related organizations.

The Fight That Yuvraj Singh Is Putting Up Against Cancer

Yuvraj Singh, a legendary cricket player from India, conquered his illness and went on to found the organization that bears his name, the "Yuvraj Singh Foundation." The organization offers financial assistance to cancer sufferers, promotes the importance of early detection, and educates people about cancer. The trip that Yuvraj has taken has served as an inspiration to a lot of people and brings attention to how important it is to be aware of your health.

The Importance of Brett Lee in Deaf Cricket

Brett Lee, a former Australian fast bowler, has been a devoted supporter for the sport of cricket for the deaf. He has been a supporter of organizations such as "Deaf Cricket Australia" and "Deaf Cricket NSW," which aim to popularize the sport within the community of hearing-impaired individuals and increase awareness of their skills.

The Initiatives for the Preservation of Rhinos by Kevin Pietersen

Kevin Pietersen, a former cricketer for England, has been very active in rhino conservation initiatives in South Africa. He utilizes his platform to bring attention to the crisis of poaching and to generate funds for the protection of these endangered creatures.

The Cricket for Good Initiative Organized by UNICEF

The 'Cricket for Good' initiative of UNICEF works in collaboration with major cricket competitions such as the ICC Cricket World Cup to raise money for charitable causes that support children. Cricketers, in their capacity as UNICEF ambassadors, engage in meaningful interaction with children, strive to improve the rights and well-being of young people, and create moments that children will remember forever.

The Obstacles and the Criticisms

The pursuit of commercialization while maintaining a focus on profits

The increasing commercialization of cricket has given rise to questions over the genuineness and purity of the sport. Some people believe that the pursuit of riches should not take precedence over the social issues that cricket may be supporting, but others disagree. Because of its increased commercialization, cricket may become more difficult to play for people of lower socioeconomic status.

Variations in the Amount of Impact

The influence of cricket on various social issues varies considerably from country to country. Cricket is a potent instrument for social change in countries like India, but it is possible that it does not have the same level of influence in other countries that play cricket. The allocation of opportunities and resources is likewise unequal, which contributes to the further widening of the gap.

Disparities Between the Sexes

There are still major gender gaps in terms of salary, recognition, and opportunity in cricket, despite the fact that women's cricket has made tremendous strides forward in recent years. It is imperative that efforts be made to resolve these inequalities and guarantee that the sport's power is utilized for the benefit of all involved parties.

The influence that cricket has on society extends well beyond the boundary ropes, which makes it an effective forum for discussing important societal problems. Promoting health, education, gender equality, and inclusiveness are some of the goals that have been advanced via the use of cricket's unifying force, worldwide reach, and the influence of its players. Cricket continues to be a driving force for social change, inspiring constructive action and serving as a light of hope in a world beset with obstacles, despite the difficulties and critiques that have been leveled against the sport. Cricket will continue to be a tremendous catalyst for positive change and a monument to the transformational potential of sport so long as it maintains its commitment to tackling social issues. This will be the case so long as the sport continues to play.

6.3 Philanthropic efforts by cricket organizations and players

The sport of cricket, which has a vast fan base and is popular all over the world, has become a key platform for philanthropic and charity activities in recent years. Cricket clubs, franchises, and players have all come to appreciate the power that comes with their influence and resources, and as a result, they have become actively involved in a diverse range of philanthropic endeavors that try to address a variety of social, economic, and environmental concerns. In this essay, we explore the philanthropic landscape of cricket and highlight the numerous initiatives taken by cricket organizations and players to generate a good and long-lasting impact on society.

Initiatives Taken by Cricket Organizations to Help the Community

Cricket organizations have been extremely instrumental in launching and supporting a wide variety of philanthropic activities, making effective use of their institutional reach and resources to tackle a variety of urgent social challenges. These activities are a manifestation of their dedication to social responsibility as well as their understanding of the sport's capacity to act as a driver of social transformation.

Programs for the Advancement of the Community

Community development projects have been formed by cricket groups with the goal of empowering underserved areas through improved access to education, health care, and athletics. These projects frequently include activities like the construction of schools, the provision of access to clean water and sanitation facilities, and the raising of knowledge on health and hygiene practices.

The Promotion of Talent at the Local Level and Its Detection

Cricket groups regularly invest in talent discovery and grassroots development programs, particularly in areas that have limited access to resources and training facilities. Young people who are interested in playing cricket have the opportunity to participate in these programs, which provide them the chance to receive expert instruction, gain access to appropriate equipment, and play in competitive settings.

Fostering Acceptance of Differences and Community

Many groups within the sport of cricket have launched initiatives in recent years in response to the growing awareness of the value of diversity and inclusion. These initiatives seek to promote gender equality and social inclusion. These efforts are centered on the goal of giving women and individuals from underserved communities equal opportunity to participate in cricket and other activities related to the sport.

Conservation of the Environment and Long-Term Sustainability

Several cricket groups have been more proactive than others in their efforts to promote environmental sustainability and conservation. Initiatives such as promoting eco-friendly stadiums, establishing waste management systems, and sponsoring reforestation initiatives demonstrate their dedication to protecting the environment and reducing the sport's overall impact on the environment.

Help for Those in Need and Other Humanitarian Causes

During times of natural disasters and other types of calamities, cricket organizations frequently organize the collection of resources and the provision of humanitarian aid. They demonstrate their responsiveness to global calamities through their collaboration with relief organizations in order to supply necessary supplies, medical help, and other types of support to communities that have been affected.

Donations Made by Cricket Players: Going Above and Beyond the Sport

In their capacity as important characters and role models, cricketers have taken advantage of the platform and resources afforded to them to participate in a variety of charitable endeavors.

Their dedication to helping those in need and improving the quality of life for those who are disadvantaged has been the impetus behind a number of significant initiatives that have had a positive impact.

Creating Foundations for Nonprofit Organizations

In order to address certain social causes that are close to their hearts, a number of cricketers have created their own philanthropic foundations. These foundations place their emphasis on issues like as education, healthcare, the reduction of poverty, and community development in an effort to produce solutions that are both sustainable and long-term for the problems that face society.

Campaigns and Events for Fundraising Purposes

Cricketers frequently organize fundraising campaigns and events in order to garner support for a variety of philanthropic causes and collect funding for those causes. These events consist of charity matches, auctions, and social media campaigns, all of which not only raise awareness about significant social concerns but also mobilize financial resources to help address such issues.

Campaigns for Advocacy and Raising Awareness

Cricketers frequently make use of their power in order to advocate for social causes and raise awareness about important topics. They take an active involvement in public campaigns, educational projects, and media engagements in order to encourage conversations and actions on themes such as health, education, gender equality, and environmental conservation.

Participation in and empowerment of the community

Cricket players frequently interact face to face with local communities, particularly those residing in disadvantaged regions, in order to offer support and facilitate empowerment. Through the means of cricket, they frequently host coaching clinics, motivational speeches, and skill development workshops with the intention of encouraging and uplifting individuals, particularly the younger generation.

Help for Those Who Are in Need, Especially Those Who Are Vulnerable

Orphaned children, people with disabilities, and survivors of domestic violence are among the underserved and vulnerable populations that receive help from a number of cricketers. They work along with philanthropic groups to supply these underserved communities with financial support, educational opportunities, and access to crucial resources.

Evaluation of the Impact and Examples of Success

One may see the impact of the charitable work done by cricket organizations and players by looking at the many success stories and positive results that have occurred as a result. These projects have resulted in measurable changes in the lives of individuals and communities, which has fostered a sense of hope, resilience, and development in those who have benefited from them.

Education and Training Leading to Professional Growth

There have been many educational programs that have been funded by cricket organizations and players, and these activities have led to higher literacy rates as well as better access to quality education in underprivileged communities. Students have been given the opportunity to pursue higher education and acquire skills that are vital for their professional development thanks to programs that provide vocational training, infrastructure development, and scholarships.

A Good State of Health and Well-Being

In areas that are underserved, improvements in healthcare access, illness prevention, and health awareness have been made possible as a result of philanthropic interventions with a focus on health and well-being. Promoting public health and treating the health issues that are most prevalent in these areas have been important goals of the medical camps, immunization drives, and awareness initiatives that have taken place recently.

Empowerment of Women and Strides Toward Gender Parity

The efforts that have been made by cricket players and organizations to promote gender equality and women's empowerment have led to an increase in the number of women participating in sports and other fields that have historically been dominated by males. These activities have helped to develop an environment that is more inclusive and egalitarian, which has given women the ability to pursue their dreams and challenge the conventions of society.

Conservation of the Environment and Long-Term Sustainability

Cricket organizations have made a contribution to the development of sustainable and environmentally friendly practices within the sport thanks to the environmental conservation activities that they have undertaken. They have set an example for fostering environmental stewardship and lowering the ecological impact of the sport by using technologies that are efficient in terms of the use of energy, techniques for the management of trash, and initiatives involving green infrastructure.

Challenges, as well as Future Things to Consider

In spite of the enormous progress that cricket organizations and players have made in terms of philanthropy, a number of problems still exist, which have an impact on the long-term viability and scalability of their projects. It is absolutely necessary to address these difficulties and think about future tactics for increasing the positive impact that charity may have in the world of cricket.

Distribution of Resources and Environmental Viability

A difficulty that continues to face cricket organizations and players is ensuring the most efficient use of available resources and the continued viability of charitable initiatives over the long term. In order to maintain charitable activities throughout time in the face of limited resources, competing goals, and constantly shifting socioeconomic factors, it is necessary to engage in strategic planning and efficient management.

Working Together and Forming Partnerships

It is possible to increase the influence and reach of charitable endeavors by fortifying alliances and partnerships with governmental agencies, non-profit organizations, and business groups. Strategic alliances can make it easier to combine resources, skills, and networks in order to more effectively handle complex societal problems.

Measurement of Impact and Openness to Feedback

It is absolutely necessary, in order to guarantee accountability and transparency, to put in place comprehensive monitoring and evaluation processes in order to evaluate the effects of charitable interventions. Cricket players and organizations need to implement transparent reporting procedures and data-driven evaluation methods in order to accurately measure the impact and outcomes of their charitable efforts.

Efforts Made to Reduce Social Differences and Inequalities

It is vital, in order to create a philanthropy ecosystem within cricket that is more inclusive and equitable, to address the underlying social imbalances and inequalities that exist. To guarantee that philanthropic projects contribute to sustained social transformation and systemic change, the focus of efforts should be on strengthening vulnerable populations, decreasing gender inequities, and encouraging diversity.

Outreach and advocacy on a global scale

It is possible to magnify the positive effects that generosity has on a wider scale by extending the global reach of cricket organizations and players and increasing the amount of advocacy work they do.

A worldwide community that is devoted to social change and sustainable development can be fostered by utilizing digital platforms, social media, and international alliances to facilitate greater awareness, involvement, and support for charitable projects.

The charitable efforts of cricket organizations and players have proved the transformative power of sports in the context of tackling difficult social concerns and generating good change in society. Their dedication to social responsibility, community empowerment, and sustainable development exemplifies cricket's ability to go beyond the confines of the sport and have a significant influence on the lives of both individuals and communities. As charity in the realm of cricket continues to develop and expand, it has the ability to leave a lasting legacy that extends beyond the confines of the sport in the form of good change, resilience, and hope.

Chapter 7

Challenges and Controversies

The sport of cricket, which is frequently referred to as the "gentleman's game," is not exempt from difficulties and debates. However, despite the fact that the sport has millions of devoted followers all over the world, it has been plagued by a number of problems, both on and off the field. This essay investigates the problems and debates that have arisen in the world of cricket, focusing on the more negative aspects that require attention and potential solutions.

Obstacles in the Game of Cricket

The sport of cricket is confronted with a number of issues that have an effect not just on the game but also on its players and the larger cricketing community. These difficulties can be broken down into three primary categories: those that occur on the field, those that occur off the field, and those that occur in administrative areas.

Obstacles Confronted While Playing

Collusion in Fixing Matches and Corruption

In cricket, match-fixing and corruption are two of the most serious difficulties that the sport faces. A number of scandals involving players, team officials, and even umpires have surfaced over the years, ruining the sport's reputation and making it less respectable to watch. Players have frequently been enticed to participate in match-fixing, spot-fixing, and other unethical actions by the prospect of financial gain as well as by the influence of illicit bookmakers. A number of different matches, both domestic and international, have been investigated, which has resulted in suspensions, bans, and legal measures being taken against players and officials.

Addiction to Substances and Doping

Another issue that has arisen on the field of play in cricket is that of doping and substance abuse. There have been cases where players have tested positive for prohibited substances, despite the fact that the sport is not as susceptible to doping as some of the other sports. Not only may doping be harmful to the health of the participants, but it can also undermine the legitimacy of the competition and compromise its standards.

Tampering with the ball

In cricket, there have been cases of players attempting to change the condition of the cricket ball in order to gain an edge. This practice, known as "ball-tampering," is a sensitive matter. In recent years, there have been a number of high-profile examples of ball-tampering that have resulted in suspensions and bans for the players involved. These cases have garnered a substantial amount of attention. The issue surrounding the manipulation of the ball pushes the limits of sportsmanship and fair play in the game of cricket.

Errors Made by the Umpires

In the sport of cricket, umpiring decisions have traditionally been a source of debate. Even though the sport has made efforts to improve umpiring standards with the implementation of technologies like as the Decision Review System (DRS), umpiring errors can still have a substantial impact on the outcome of a match. When teams believe that they have been on the receiving end of wrong rulings, disputes and controversies frequently occur.

Problems Away From the Field

Concerns Regarding the Behavior and Conduct of Players

An additional difficulty that occurs off the field in the sport of cricket is player behavior and conduct. The reputation of the sport has been tarnished as a result of instances of players engaging in improper conduct on the playing field. These incidents include verbal abuse, sledging, and physical altercations. The governing authorities of cricket face a continuing problem in the form of ensuring that players continue to uphold high standards of sportsmanship and discipline.

Concerns Regarding the Behavior of Fans, as well as Their Safety

The behavior of cricket supporters, both inside and outside of the stadiums, can present difficulties for those in charge of the sport's administration. Matches have been disrupted as a result of incidents of crowd disruptions, pitch invasions, and even acts of violence, which has prompted security concerns. An vital yet frequently problematic aspect of planning cricket matches is doing so in a manner that protects both the participants and the spectators.

The Scheduling and the Exhaustion of the Players

Concerns regarding player weariness and burnout have arisen as a result of the packed international schedule of cricket and the growing popularity of Twenty20 leagues. The most accomplished players on the international stage frequently compete in several game formats throughout the entire year. This hectic playing schedule can easily result in injuries as well as mental tiredness. It is a never-ending struggle to find a happy medium between preserving the economic viability of the game and looking out for the health and safety of its participants.

Inequitable Division of Available Resources

A fundamental difficulty that occurs outside the field of play in cricket is the unequal distribution of resources. Smaller nations that play cricket have a harder time competing on an even playing field than the main cricket-playing nations do since the major nations have access to enormous financial and infrastructure resources. This difference has the potential to stymie the expansion and development of the sport in developing nations that play cricket.

Challenges in the Administration

Governance and Openness to Information

The governing authorities of cricket have struggled with challenges relating to governance and transparency. Allegations of corruption, nepotism, and a lack of transparency in decision-making processes are among the administrative issues that organizations face today. These challenges have the potential to damage the legitimacy of cricket boards and to break the public's trust.

Conflicts and Battles in the Courts

The administration of cricket has been beset by legal conflicts and disagreements. Court fights can sometimes be expected to last for an extended period of time when disagreements arise around broadcast rights, franchise ownership, and organizational structures. These disagreements have the potential to divert money and attention away from the sport's continued expansion and development.

Potentially Conflicting Interests

The administrators of cricket have struggled with problems including conflicts of interest. Instances within the ecosystem of cricketing in which individuals simultaneously occupy numerous positions, such as being team owners, selectors, and board members have generated issues over impartiality and fair decision-making.

Cricket's Most Contentious Issues

Over the course of its history, cricket has also been involved in its fair share of scandals. These debates range in scope from specific problems with the game to more systemic difficulties with society as a whole.

Tampering with the Ball Scandals

Cricket has been shaken by controversies involving ball-tampering, which has spurred arguments about ethics and sportsmanship.

The infamous "Sandpaper Gate" event that occurred during a test match in South Africa in 2018 featuring Australian cricketers David Warner, Steve Smith, and Cameron Bancroft resulted in sanctions and public indignation against the players involved. The incident brought to light the pressure and desperation that athletes can experience when playing in an atmosphere with a high level of competition.

The match-fixing scandal that rocked the Indian Premier League (IPL)

A match-fixing scandal rocked the Indian Premier League (IPL) in 2013, making headlines throughout the world as one of the most watched Twenty20 tournaments. As a consequence of the allegations of spot-fixing that were leveled against a number of cricket players and team officials, they were suspended and legal action was taken. The incident brought to light flaws in both the governance of the league and the behavior of its players.

Controversies Involving the Umpires

In cricket, controversial decisions made by umpires have been an ongoing problem. Notable examples include the Sydney Test that took place in 2008 between Australia and India. During that match, there were a number of contentious decisions made, which ultimately contributed to tensions between the two teams. Errors made by umpires can open the door to allegations of favoritism and generate passionate responses from players and supporters.

There have been accusations of racism and bias

The sport of cricket has not been able to avoid accusations of prejudice and bigotry. A number of players, as well as opponents, fans, and even umpires, have been accused by other players of engaging in discriminatory behavior based on race or nationality. The widespread problems of exclusion and unequal treatment that exist within the sport have been brought to light as a result of these instances.

Player Conduct and Corrective Actions are Discussed Here

In the sport of cricket, player behavior and the use of disciplinary measures have frequently been the focus of debate. Arguments concerning the place of aggression and sportsmanship in the game have been provoked by incidents in which players have tussled with one another on the playing field or violated the code of conduct for the sport.

Scandals in the financial sector and poor management

Numerous cricket boards and organizations have been impacted by scandals and mismanagement involving their finances. Legal inquiries and administrative turmoil have been caused in cricketing bodies as a result of allegations of financial irregularities, misappropriation of funds, and corruption in financial matters.

Taking on Difficulties and Controversies

The efforts that are made to address the difficulties and controversies in cricket need to adopt a multi-faceted strategy that involves all of the relevant stakeholders. These stakeholders include cricket boards, players, fans, and the media. The following is a list of potential solutions to these problems:

Measures to combat corruption should be beefed up

Cricket boards need to keep investing in integrity and anti-corruption units of sufficient strength. A comprehensive education on the hazards of match-fixing and corruption should be provided to players and officials, and there should be clear punishments for infractions of the rules. Transparency and working cooperatively with law enforcement agencies are also necessary components of an effective response to these concerns.

Encourage Good Sportsmanship as well as Fair Play

The governing authorities of cricket ought to make encouraging sportsmanship and fair play their top priority. A stringent set of disciplinary sanctions should be in place for those players who violate the code of conduct, and the players should be held accountable for their behavior both on and off the field. It is possible to contribute to the development of a culture of respect within a sport by spreading awareness about the concepts of sportsmanship.

Take Action Against Unruly Fans

Misbehavior on the part of spectators should be addressed collaboratively by stadium officials, security personnel, and cricket boards. Every guest will have a better chance of staying safe and having a good time if adequate security precautions are taken, the stadium's laws are strictly enforced, and public awareness initiatives are carried out.

Concerns for both the Scheduling and the Health of the Players

It is important to put player wellness first while also attempting to strike a balance in the cricket schedule. This includes ensuring that players have access to sports science and medical support, controlling the demands of the players, and giving proper rest periods. When planning the schedules of both international and domestic competitions, organizers must to take participants' physical and mental health into account.

Foster an inclusive environment and equal opportunity

The governing bodies of cricket ought to take proactive steps to promote inclusiveness and equitable opportunity within the sport. In order to accomplish this, avenues need to be created for women and individuals from backgrounds underrepresented in cricket to participate in the sport, either as players or administrators. Taking a systematized approach to addressing these concerns can be facilitated by putting in place diversity and inclusion policies.

Reforms of the Governance System

Reforms to governance should be implemented by cricket's regulating bodies in order to raise the sport's openness, accountability, and ethical standards. Restoring the public's faith in cricket administration can be aided by the implementation of independent scrutiny and the separation of responsibilities aimed at preventing conflicts of interest.

Utilization of Technology in the Officiating Process

It is recommended that the use of technology, such as the Decision Review System (DRS), be expanded in order to reduce the number of disputed judgments and umpiring errors. This has the potential to improve the accuracy of rulings and reduce the number of disputes that occur during matches.

Education and a Raising of Awareness

Education and awareness programs should be run for players, referees, and fans to heighten their understanding of the repercussions of bigotry, racism, and disruptive behavior. It is essential for there to be a culture in cricket that values diversity and respect for others.

The game of cricket is not an exception to the rule that contests and debates are inherently ingrained in the nature of all sports. Even though the sport has provided millions of followers with indescribable happiness and excitement, it has also been plagued by problems that have called its integrity, sportsmanship, and governance into question. It is necessary for cricket boards, players, fans, and other stakeholders to actively participate in order to address these difficulties and controversies because they are a shared duty that must be addressed. It is essential that continued efforts be made to preserve the ethos of cricket as a "gentleman's game," to promote fairness, diversity, and transparency, and to guarantee the welfare of players if the sport is to continue to serve as a source of motivation and enjoyment for future generations. Cricket has the potential to emerge stronger and more resilient if it recognizes these issues and makes concerted efforts to address them. In doing so, the sport will demonstrate its capacity to triumph over hardship while preserving its cherished traditions and ideals.

7.1 Match-fixing scandals and their impact on the game

Cricket, which is commonly known as the "gentleman's game," has been tainted by a slew of match-fixing scandals that have rattled the sport's roots and tarnished its reputation in recent years. Players, officials, and illegal bookies are all implicated in these incidents because they conspired to influence the results of games for financial advantage by manipulating the outcomes. This essay goes into the murky realm of cricket match-fixing scandals, analyzing their origins, the fallout from them, and the ongoing fight to rid the sport of this problem.

Comprehending the Practice of Match-Fixing in Cricket

Spot-fixing is the process of manipulating particular components of a game, such as the number of no-balls or wide deliveries in a given over, the timing of wickets, or the total number of runs scored in an innings.

Fixing a match involves altering the outcome of an entire match by having players purposefully underperform or engaging in techniques that favor one team over another.

Manipulating the conditions of the playing field or the weather in order to give one team an unfair advantage in a match is an example of one type of match-fixing known as "pitch and weather manipulation."

Complicity on the Part of Players and Umpires Players or umpires may work together with illicit bookies or fixers to attempt to affect the outcome of the game.

Scandals involving match-fixing are almost always motivated by financial considerations. Unregulated bookmakers give players and officials access to huge quantities of money in exchange for their participation in manipulating matches. These bookies, who are frequently involved in organized crime, put bets on the projected outcomes, and when their plans are successful, they gain huge profits from those bets.

Match-Fixing Scandals of Notable Proportions in the Sport of Cricket

The Hansie Cronje Scandal (2000): The involvement of South African captain Hansie Cronje in match-fixing was brought to light when transcripts of discussions between him and an Indian bookmaker were exposed. The scandal was known as "The Cronje Affair." After admitting to receiving money to influence the outcome of matches, Cronje was permanently disqualified from the sport of cricket.

A Scandal Involving the Fixing of Spots in Pakistan (2010): During a test match between Pakistan and England, it was discovered that three of the Pakistani players, namely Salman Butt, Mohammad Asif, and Mohammad Amir, had engaged in match-fixing. They agreed among themselves to bowl deliberate no-balls at predetermined intervals. The three players were each subject to suspensions and legal repercussions.

The Match-Fixing Scandal that Engulfed the Indian Premier League (2013) The Indian Premier League (IPL) was engulfed in a match-fixing scandal when players from the Rajasthan Royals club were suspected of taking money to underperform in particular matches. In connection with the affair, a number of cricket players and bookmakers were taken into custody.

The Scandal Regarding the Bangladesh Premier League (BPL) (2016): There have been suspicions of match-fixing in the Bangladesh Premier tournament (BPL), which is the country's primary Twenty20 tournament. Several players, including international cricketers, have been accused in plots to control the results of matches.

The influence that match-fixing scandals have had on cricket

Loss of Confidence in the Public System

The public's trust in cricket suffers as a direct result of match-fixing allegations. When sports fans learn that the outcomes of games are influenced for financial advantage, it can leave them feeling deceived and let down, especially if they have an emotional investment in the game. This breach of confidence has the potential to have an enduring effect on the attractiveness of the sport as well as its potential for financial success.

Integrity of the Sport Has Been Compromised

When match-fixing allegations become public knowledge, the sport of cricket's credibility is put in jeopardy. The foundation of the sport is centered on ethics such as fair play, good sportsmanship, and healthy competition. The manipulation of matches undermines these standards and casts a shade on the fundamental values of the game.

Damage to One's Reputation

Cricketing boards, individual players, and officials, as well as teams, can have their reputations damaged by controversies involving match-fixing. Cricket players who are found guilty of match-fixing face considerable personal and professional fall-out, including permanent bans from the sport, legal penalties, and possible criminal prosecution.

Consequences for the Law

When a match is fixed, it is common for players, officials, and bookies to face legal repercussions for their involvement in illicit actions. These repercussions can include criminal prosecution. Legal procedures are notoriously time-consuming and resource-intensive, which frequently results in drawn-out fights in the courts.

Repercussions on one's finances

As a result of match-fixing allegations, cricket's sponsors and broadcasters may reevaluate their relationship with the sport. The loss of financial assistance from commercial entities can have major repercussions for cricket boards' finances and limit their capacity to make investments in the expansion and improvement of the sport.

Influence on Newly Emerged Players

Recent incidents involving match-fixing have made young and aspiring cricket players wary about making a career in the sport. Talented individuals may be dissuaded from pursuing a career in the sport if they are concerned that they may become involved in corrupt activities.

Complications for the Player-Board Relationships

Scandals involving match-fixing almost always result in tense relations between the players and the cricket boards. Players may believe that their boards are not providing enough support or protection for them, while boards may experience a sense of betrayal as a result of the behavior of the individuals involved.

Reforms in Regulatory Agencies and Corporate Governance

Scandals involving match-fixing frequently lead to regulatory and governance changes being implemented by cricket boards and organizations. These changes are being made with the intention of bolstering anti-corruption measures and ensuring that decision-making procedures are open and honest.

Efforts Made to Combat Fixing of Matches

Organizaciones Anticorrupción

Anti-corruption units have been established by the majority of cricket boards in order to monitor and investigate any questionable actions. In their efforts to weed out corruption, these units educate players on the perils of match-fixing, undertake surveillance, and liaise with law enforcement agencies.

Standards of Behavior and Ethical Conduct

The governing bodies of cricket have instituted stringent codes of conduct and ethics for players, officials, and other stakeholders in the game. These codes specify what kinds of behaviors are permissible and lay out the consequences for violating them.

Education and a Consciousness Effort

Players are educated about the dangers and repercussions of match-fixing through the implementation of various education and awareness programs. The players are educated to spot and report any suspicious behavior by the fixers who approach them.

Application of Techniques

The use of technology, such as the Decision Review System (DRS), has become more widespread in an effort to cut down on the number of mistakes made by the umpires and lower the risk of game-fixing. Monitoring betting trends and spotting abnormalities both benefit from the use of technology in their respective analysis processes.

Cooperation with judicial and law enforcement authorities

Investigations into claims of match-fixing are conducted in conjunction with law enforcement agencies by cricket governing bodies and anti-corruption teams. As a result of this cooperation, persons who were involved in fixing have been apprehended and convicted.

Protection for People Who Whistleblower

Whistleblowers who come out with information concerning match-fixing have been the target of efforts that have been made to safeguard them. Individuals are encouraged to disclose illegal or unethical conduct by whistleblower protection schemes, which alleviate their fears of retaliation.

Regulations that are more stringent for franchise leagues

More stringent procedures have been implemented by domestic Twenty20 leagues like the Indian Premier League (IPL) in an effort to curb match-fixing and spot-fixing. These leagues are being closely examined to make certain that they uphold the greatest possible levels of integrity in their operations.

The integrity of the sport, its reputation, and its future are all at jeopardy as a result of match-fixing incidents, which have cast a shadow over cricket. These scandals have resulted in the erosion of public trust, the destruction of reputations, and legal repercussions for individuals who were involved. Positive outcomes have been achieved, however, as a result of the combined efforts made by the cricketing community to prevent match-fixing through anti-corruption measures, education, and technology.

The capacity of cricket to recover from scandalous situations demonstrates the sport's resiliency in combating match-fixing and its dedication to protecting the essential values of the sport. The integrity of cricket and the public's trust in the sport are of the utmost importance, thus the sport must continue to adapt while maintaining its vigilance in its ongoing battle against match-fixing.

Cricket has the potential to overcome the obstacles faced by match-fixing and maintain its ability to inspire millions of fans all around the world if collaborative action, transparency, and an uncompromising adherence to ethical standards are implemented.

7.2 Corruption and power struggles within cricket administration

Within its administrative structures, the sport of cricket, which is commonly referred to as the "gentleman's game," has been plagued by instances of corruption and power struggles. There have been occasions when the very institutions that are responsible for governing and promoting the sport have been mired in scandals and conflicts, which has caused the integrity of the game to be called into question. This essay goes deep into the murky world of power conflicts and corruption that exists inside the administration of cricket. It sheds light on the reasons why these problems exist, the effects they have, and the attempts that are being made to solve them.

Administration of Cricket marred by Corruption

The misappropriation of financial resources that were intended for the growth of the sport, which ultimately results in losses and financial instability. This practice is known as "embezzlement of funds."

Nepotism refers to the practice of giving appointments in the cricketing industry to family members, acquaintances, or close allies rather than on the basis of merit or transparency.

Accepting illicit payments, gifts, or kickbacks from stakeholders such as broadcasters,

advertisers, or franchise owners in exchange for favorable decisions is an example of a corrupt practice known as "kickbacks" or "bribes."

Manipulating the voting and election processes within cricket boards in order to acquire

influential positions and keep control of the sport is an example of vote manipulation.

Individuals who simultaneously fulfill various responsibilities in the administration of cricket, such as being team owners, selectors, and board members, might put themselves in a position where they have competing interests. This is known as a conflict of interest.

Exploiting players by undervaluing or overvaluing their contracts, typically for the benefit of particular individuals or parties, is an example of poor player contract management.

Corruption within the administration of cricket damages the integrity of the sport, erodes public trust, and has far-reaching ramifications for both the game and its various stakeholders.

Conflicts about authority within the Cricket Administration

Political Factions: Within cricket boards and organizations, different factions struggle with one another for control and influence, which can lead to conflict within the organization.

Rival areas within a country might compete with one another for representation and authority, which can lead to divides and complicate the decision-making process.

Influence of Third Parties Third parties, like as influential persons or groups, may attempt to use their position to exert an inappropriate amount of influence on the cricket administration in order to forward their own agendas.

Leadership Conflicts It is possible for disputes and conflicts to occur among cricket's leaders and executives regarding the sport's overall direction and governance.

Power struggles can arise from a variety of reasons, one of which is the struggle to maintain control over the distribution and administration of available financial resources.

Power clashes During Elections Elections for important positions within cricket boards can lead to intense and sometimes contentious power clashes. Elections can be a battlefield.

The Repercussions of Bribery and Power Struggles

Loss of Confidence in the Public System

The public's trust in cricket administration is being eroded by instances of corruption and power disputes. When participants, fans, and sponsors believe that personal agendas and political considerations are given more weight than those of the sport itself, they experience a growing sense of disillusionment.

The Cricket Brand Suffered Some Damage

When allegations of corruption and power conflicts inside the administration of cricket are brought to light, the sport's reputation takes a hit. This damage extends to the reputation of the sport as a whole as well as the sport's capacity to uphold the ideals that it holds dear.

Mismanagement of the Financial Resources

Corruption can result in poor management of financial resources, which in turn can lead to financial instability and reduce a sport's capacity to invest in its future expansion and improvement.

Unhappiness among the Players

Players' dissatisfaction, as well as their morale and performance on the field, can be negatively impacted by power struggles and conflicts that occur inside the administration of cricket. There is a possibility that participants will feel as though their interests are not being effectively represented.

A Blockade to Progress and Development

At the grassroots level of the sport, corruption and power disputes can be obstacles to the sport's development. There is a possibility of loss of investment in areas like as infrastructure, coaching, and the development of talent.

Consequences for the Law

Individuals who engage in unethical behavior and are found to be corrupt within the cricket administration frequently face legal repercussions, including the possibility of being charged with a crime and subjected to judicial processes.

Efforts Made to Tackle Corruption as Well as Power Struggles

Reforms of the Governance System

Reforms in governance should be implemented by cricket boards and organizations with the goals of raising the sport's level of openness, accountability, and ethical standards. These changes have the potential to restore public trust while also preventing power struggles and corruption.

Free and Separate Oversight

The acts of the cricket administration can be monitored and evaluated with the assistance of independent oversight groups. This helps to ensure that decisions are made with the best interests of the sport in mind, rather than for the sake of individual benefit.

Policies Regarding Potential Conflicts of Interest

Cricket boards ought to institute stringent conflict of interest regulations to prohibit individuals from having numerous jobs, which could undermine the quality of their decision-making.

Protection for People Who Whistleblower

Whistleblowers are people who come forward with knowledge regarding corrupt and unethical practices inside the administration of cricket. Efforts should be taken to protect people who do this. Individuals are encouraged to denounce corrupt practices without fear of punishment because to measures that protect those who blow the whistle.

Improving the Capacity of Ethics Committees

Cricket organizations ought to form or bolster ethics committees with the responsibility of

investigating and addressing complaints of unethical behavior and corruption.

Instructional Methods and Programs

Education and training programs should be conducted for persons involved in the administration of cricket. The goal of these programs is to create knowledge about ethical standards and the consequences of unethical behavior.

Elections that are Open and Honest

The likelihood of power struggles and electoral disputes can be mitigated if cricket boards take measures to guarantee that elections for key posts are carried out in a transparent manner and in compliance with the procedures that have been set.

The integrity of the sport of cricket, along with its reputation, is under considerable danger due to the presence of corruption and power struggles inside the administration of the sport. These problems have far-reaching implications, as they affect public trust, financial stability, player morale, and the evolution of the game. In order to overcome these obstacles, cricket needs to put more emphasis on governance improvements, increased openness, and higher ethical standards.

It is essential for the sport to demonstrate resiliency in the face of corruption and power conflicts if it is to continue to keep its fundamental ideals and continue to hold its place as the gentleman's game. Cricket can continue to excite millions of fans all over the world and can develop an environment in which the best interests of the sport take precedence over personal gain and power conflicts if everyone involved in the sport works together to root out and eradicate corruption and promote transparency.

7.3 Ethical dilemmas and cricket's response to social challenges

Cricket is much more than just a sport; it is a global phenomenon that brings together millions of individuals from all kinds of different backgrounds. Due to the game's extensive history, traditions, and ideals, it has become an important component of the social fabric in a number of different countries. Cricket, however, is not immune to the ethical conundrums and the problems given by social issues; it is much like any other realm of human endeavor in this regard. This essay investigates the different moral conundrums that cricket has had to deal with over the course of its history, as well as the ways in which the sport has responded to various societal difficulties.

1. **Ethical Conundrums Facing the Sport of Cricket**
Fixing of matches and general corruption

The problem of match-fixing and corruption is one of the most significant ethical conundrums that cricket has ever been forced to contend with. This problem first came to light in the early 2000s when a number of prominent players, like as Hansie Cronje and Mohammad Azharuddin, were accused of fixing matches. This brought the issue to the forefront of public attention. The exposure of these scandals sent shockwaves across the cricketing community and brought into doubt the sport's reputation for fair play.

As a response, the authorities in charge of cricket instituted stringent anti-corruption measures, one of which was the formation of the Anti-Corruption and Security Unit (ACSU) by the International Cricket Council (ICC). The aim of the Anti-Corruption and Security Unit (ACSU) is to monitor and investigate suspicious activity while also working to educate players, authorities, and other stakeholders about the dangers of corruption. Even though these safeguards have been somewhat successful in reducing instances of corruption, the possibility of match-fixing is still present, and cricket is still struggling to find a solution to this ethical conundrum.

The use of performance-enhancing drugs as well as doping

Doping and the use of performance-enhancing chemicals provide another difficulty from an ethical standpoint in cricket. Even though the physical requirements of playing cricket are lower than those of other sports, players are nevertheless expected to provide their very best effort. Because of this, there have been cases where players have turned to doping in order to obtain a competitive advantage.

Cricket authorities, including the International Cricket Council (ICC), have instituted anti-doping measures in accordance with the laws established by the World Anti-Doping Agency (WADA).

A random drug test, education programs for players, and penalties for those who are discovered to be using performance-enhancing drugs are all included in these policies. The objective is to safeguard the well-being of the players while also preserving the honor of the competition.

Discrimination Based on Race

Discrimination on the basis of race has been an ongoing problem in the sport of cricket for a very long time, notably in the context of South Africa and the West Indies. During the time of apartheid in South Africa, a racially divided cricket structure existed, and black players were not allowed to participate on the national team. On the field of play in the West Indies, racial conflicts between players hailing from various islands occasionally bubbled to the surface.

The governing bodies of cricket have taken some measures to combat the problem of racial prejudice in the sport. In the 1990s, South Africa made a huge stride toward overcoming the legacy of apartheid by rejoining international cricket competition. This was an important move. A difficult subject, the establishment of quotas to ensure representation of players from previously disadvantaged backgrounds has been an attempt to right past injustices. Quotas have been implemented in order to ensure that players from previously disadvantaged backgrounds are represented.

Equality of the sexes

Inequality between the sexes has also been a big ethical problem in the sport of cricket. Throughout its history, the game of cricket played by women has received a significantly lower level of attention, funding, and recognition than the game played by men. In spite of this, over the course of the past few years, the women's cricket team has made great progress in terms of professionalization, visibility, and chances.

The International Cricket Council (ICC) has been instrumental in advancing women's cricket through a number of initiatives, including the organization of the Women's World Cup and the World Twenty20, the provision of equal prize money for men's and women's competitions, and the backing of grassroots development programs for girls. In spite of all of these efforts, there is still a significant distance to travel before gender equality can be achieved in cricket.

2. **The Cricket Players Reaction to Social Difficulties**

Advancing the Values of Sportsmanship and Fair Play

The game of cricket has dealt with its share of moral conundrums by putting an emphasis on the virtues of sportsmanship and fair play. These principles are encapsulated in the spirit of cricket, which was most memorably articulated by Colin Cowdrey, a former president of the MCC.

It instills a sense of healthy competition among players while simultaneously fostering an attitude of fair play and respect for one another. Players including cricket Sir Don Bradman, Sachin Tendulkar, and Sir Vivian Richards have been able to exemplify this spirit throughout their careers.

Efforts to Combat and Prevent Corruption

Cricket has instituted stringent anti-corruption measures, such as codes of conduct, education programs, and surveillance, in an effort to combat match-fixing and corruption. The formation of the ACSU by the ICC has been an important step in this direction, and it has already had a substantial impact. There has been an increase in the emphasis placed on reporting any questionable activity, and players and authorities are also educated about the dangers of corruption.

Leadership With Integrity

The governing bodies of cricket have acknowledged the significance of having ethical leaders inside the sport. It is vital to choose people of integrity to critical posts in the administration of cricket in order to address any ethical difficulties that may arise. Governing bodies of cricket, such as the International Cricket Council (ICC) and national cricket boards, have been making attempts to recruit ethical leaders who are capable of establishing a positive tone for the sport.

Diversity and Welcoming Attitudes

Cricket has taken steps to resolve concerns relating to the inclusion and diversity of its players. The example of South Africa, where the sport of cricket was instrumental in reducing racial tensions, is instructive and motivating. In an effort to increase diversity, several initiatives, such as scholarship programs and player quotas, have been put into place. One of these initiatives is the promotion of cricket in disadvantaged communities.

Equality of the sexes

The growth of women's cricket at all levels is part of the cricket community's response to the problem of achieving gender equality. As a result of the rise in popularity of competitions such as the Women's World Cup, cricket for women is increasingly regarded as a respectable and potentially lucrative professional path. The participation of women in important administrative and decision-making roles is another step toward achieving gender equality in the sport of cricket.

Development from the Ground Up

Cricket has placed an emphasis on grass-roots development programs in order to solve the ethical and social difficulties that it faces.

These programs have the overarching goal of increasing access to the sport for underserved areas, particularly in nations that have a long history of racial or economic inequality. Cricket has the potential to aid in the dismantling of social barriers, particularly if it is taught to children at an early age and if facilities for coaching and guidance are made available.

Education and Awareness Campaigns for the Public

Education is a crucial instrument for tackling the moral conundrums and social problems that exist in the sport of cricket. It is extremely important to educate the general population on important topics such as corruption, doping, racism, and gender inequality. The fans, the players, and the other stakeholders all need to be informed and educated about the issues as well as the actions that are being taken to address those issues.

Cricket, like any other human effort, is not exempt from moral conundrums or social pressures; this is especially true in international cricket. Integrity of the sport has been undermined in important ways by a number of issues, including but not limited to: match-fixing, corruption, doping, racial prejudice, and gender inequity. However, the reaction that cricket has given to these concerns demonstrates a commitment to addressing ethical conundrums and societal challenges.

Cricket has developed anti-corruption measures, encouraged ethical leadership, and worked toward increasing diversity and inclusion. It has also placed an emphasis on values such as fair play and sportsmanship. Case studies like as the Hansie Cronje controversy, the reintegration of South Africa, the rise of women's cricket, and grass-roots development in Afghanistan highlight the sport's capacity to address ethical challenges and contribute to constructive social change. Other examples include.

The way in which cricket deals with moral conundrums and social issues will continue to be an essential component of the sport's identity and legacy even as the world in which it is played undergoes ongoing development and adaptation. Cricket has the potential to continue to be a positive force in society and a symbol of fair play and sportsmanship if it is developed at the grassroots level while also having ethical leaders that raise public awareness, educate students, and educate the public.

Chapter 8

The Future of Cricket and Social Change

Cricket, which is frequently referred to as the "gentleman's game," is no longer only a sport but rather a global phenomenon that has a significant impact on several aspects of society. As we go into a new era, the potential for social transformation on a variety of fronts is intricately entwined with the course that cricket will take in the years to come. This essay investigates the changing landscape of cricket, focusing on the obstacles and opportunities that the sport faces as well as the role that cricket may play in fostering constructive social change.

1. **The Changing Face of Cricket in the Landscape**
   The Twenty20 format: a Revolution in Cricket
   Cricket has been revolutionized by the implementation of the Twenty20 (T20) format, which was first played in the early 2000s. This format makes the sport more approachable and appealing to a wider audience. As a result of the shorter format, there is now more excitement, the games move at a faster pace, and there has been a rise in popularity. The Indian Premier League (IPL) and the Big Bash League (BBL) are two examples of leagues that have become so popular that they attract fans from all over the world.

   T20 cricket has not only boosted the financial worth of the sport but also made it more inclusive, bringing in various fan bases. This has resulted in higher revenue for the sport. It offers a platform for cricket to connect to a younger generation and to regions where the longer forms may have struggled to acquire popularity. This makes it possible for cricket to appeal to a wider audience. T20 cricket continues to dominate the scene and reinvent the dynamics of the sport, therefore it is unavoidable that it will play a significant role in the development of cricket in the future.

   The Development of Women's Cricket
   One of the most encouraging trends to emerge in cricket recently is the expansion of the game's offerings for female players. Women's cricket has progressed

from a state in which it was underfunded and underrecognized to one in which it is garnering increased attention, investment, and opportunity.

The skill and level of competition displayed by female cricket players has been brought to light as a result of the success of tournaments such as the Women's World Cup and the Women's T20 World Cup.

The Women's Twenty20 World Cup final in 2020 is expected to exceed attendance records, indicating that gender equality will play an increasingly important role in the sport's future. Women's cricket has opened up new markets and fan bases, and the continued efforts to promote and grow the women's game show that cricket's gender balance has a bright future ahead of it.

Technology as well as innovative thinking

Several facets of the sport of cricket have been profoundly altered as a result of the introduction of innovative technologies. The Decision Review System (DRS) and ball-tracking technology have both contributed to an increase in the accuracy of the decisions made by umpires. The viewer experience has been improved by to innovations such as Spidercam and Hawk-Eye, which provide a closer look at the action taking place on the field.

In addition, the use of wearable technology and data analysis have become fundamental components in the process of evaluating player performance and preventing injuries. The manner that players are trained is shifting as a result of developments in sports science and analytics, and insights powered by data are assisting teams in the process of making strategic decisions.

The continuation of technology breakthroughs, which will lead to improvements in cricket's competitiveness, entertainment value, and player performance, is essential to the sport's long-term viability.

The Internationalization of the Game

The International Cricket Council (ICC) is in charge of the sport's administration and progression, which contributes to cricket's widespread popularity around the world. The introduction of cricket in countries that do not traditionally play the game is one aspect that defines the globalization of the sport. For instance, the attempts of the International Cricket Council (ICC) to include cricket in the Olympic Games can help expand the sport to new heights and regions.

In addition, Twenty20 competitions such as the IPL have been successful in recruiting the best players from around the world, which has helped cricket become more popular in more countries than ever before.

The future of cricket as a truly global sport is being shaped by a number of factors, including the possible rise of new cricketing powerhouses and the expansion of the game's fan base in nations such as the United States of America, Canada, and the United Arab Emirates.

2. **The Role of Cricket as a Driver of Social Transformation**
Fostering Acceptance of Differences and Community
The capacity of cricket to bring people together from a wide variety of walks of life is one of the sport's most notable strengths. As the sport continues to gain popularity all around the world, it presents an important opportunity to foster inclusiveness and diversity. Cricket may serve as a model for unity and harmony if it welcomes players and fans from a diverse range of cultural backgrounds.

Players from all over the world are able to communicate with one another and build friendships despite the national and cultural differences they come from because to the worldwide reach of Twenty20 leagues. This interaction between people of different cultures has the potential to foster a greater understanding and respect for one another, both on and off the field.

Empowering Women Through Athletics
The growing popularity of women's cricket is making a significant contribution to the advancement of gender equality in athletics. Female cricket players are challenging gender norms and encouraging younger generations of girls and women to achieve their goals in an industry that has historically been controlled by men. Not only does success in women's cricket depend on winning matches, but it also requires going against the grain of societal standards.

Women can continue to gain more independence through participation in cricket if the sport gives them opportunities at every level. This empowerment extends beyond the field, as women who hold top positions in cricket administration and broadcasting are able to contribute to changing the narrative around gender roles.

Impact on Society and Development at the Local Level
The grassroots cricket development projects have the ability to bring about major social change in their respective communities. Cricket has the potential to provide a diversion from unfavorable influences and to encourage a lifestyle that is more physically active and healthful if it is played in schools and communities. These initiatives can focus on disadvantaged communities, opening doors for youngsters who

otherwise might not have the chance to participate in organized sports activities. Cricket is a great way to inculcate important life lessons, such as the importance of collaboration, discipline, and determination, which are crucial for an individual's growth and success.

Bringing Attention to Important Social Issues Through Cricket
The sport of cricket provides a platform from which to address important societal concerns such as health, education, and social inclusion. Cricketing bodies and players can contribute to causes such as disaster relief, public health, and education by organizing charity matches, fund-raising events, and awareness campaigns.

Cricket players are frequently seen as role models within their communities, and it is possible to capitalize on their influence to bring about constructive change. Players and cricket groups have raised awareness of vital issues such as mental health, domestic violence, and environmental conservation by putting light on these matters and providing help where it is required.

3. **Obstacles and Delays in Progress**

The Effect That Commercialization Has on People's Values

The tremendous financial advantages that cricket has seen as a result of its increasing commercialization can be attributed to the proliferation of Twenty20 leagues and corporate sponsorships. However, it has also given rise to concerns regarding the possible impact on the more traditional aspects of the game of cricket. When this happens, an ethical conundrum is created since people are trying to make money at the expense of the fun of the game.

The future success of cricket will be determined by how well it strikes a balance between the sport's commercial interests and the protection of its fundamental principles, which include respect, sportsmanship, and fair play.

Inequality as well as unfairness

In spite of continued efforts to broaden participation, the sport of cricket continues to struggle with unequal access to opportunities, resources, and representation. In some nations, only a few players control the landscape of cricket, while the majority of players have a difficult time gaining attention and access to resources. Pay equality, media coverage, and chances for sponsorship are all areas in which women's cricket, in particular, is struggling to make progress.

In order for cricket to truly act as a catalyst for social change, it will be necessary for these discrepancies to be overcome. These problems can be alleviated in part by implementing measures such as quotas, investing in the growth of grassroots organizations, and modifying sponsorship tactics.

Fixing of matches and general corruption

The integrity of cricket continues to be tainted by the continued presence of the risk of match-fixing and corruption. Despite the fact that anti-corruption measures have been implemented, a continuing obstacle presents itself in the form of the ever-evolving strategies employed by corrupt persons. The continuation of cricket is dependent on the game's administrators' ability to anticipate and counteract potential challenges to the sport's rules and traditions.

Education and awareness initiatives for participants, officials, and stakeholders, as well as the use of technology to detect corruption, are crucial components of this continuing effort to combat bribery and other forms of misconduct.

Player Safety and Welfare

The pressures placed on modern cricket players, particularly in formats such as Twenty20, can lead to both physical and mental health problems. Players may experience wear and tear as a result of long tours, a high number of matches, and the pressure to perform at the greatest level. To ensure that cricket players may have successful and long-lasting careers, player welfare needs to be a top focus in the sport.

The future of cricket should center on developing a scheduling system that takes into account the various requirements of the players and allows for sufficient downtime. In addition, gamers should have easy access to assistance and resources for mental health, which can assist them in coping with the demands associated with playing the game.

4. The Function of Cricket's Governing Bodies and the Leadership

Administration and Regulatory Structures

The governing bodies of cricket are responsible for ensuring that the sport's rules and regulations are just, equal, and consistent with the core principles that define cricket. This includes tackling issues such as the gender pay gap, inclusion of people of all genders, and diversity within teams and administrations.

Programs for Program Development

In order to broaden cricket's appeal and make it more accessible to new players, national cricket boards and international organizations should fund grassroots development programs. These programs ought to give precedence to disadvantaged communities and actively seek out and encourage involvement from girls and women.

The Duty to Care for Others

The governing bodies of cricket have a duty to fulfill their social responsibilities by addressing significant problems such as mental health, environmental preservation, and social inclusion. They ought to make use of their position in order to raise awareness and motivate change.

Integrity and openness are essential values.

The governing bodies of cricket are responsible for ensuring the sport's continued legitimacy by enacting and upholding stringent anti-corruption policies. Building trust and confidence among players and spectators requires a commitment to responsibility as well as transparency in decision-making processes.

Player Safety and Welfare

The welfare of the players need to be the primary priority of those in charge of cricket. They need to work together with player associations and medical specialists to make sure that the physical and emotional health of players is a top priority.

Cricket is poised to play an increasingly prominent role in creating constructive social change, which bodes well for the sport's future. The panorama of the future of cricket is dynamic and exciting. The development of Twenty20 cricket, the expansion of women's cricket, advances in technology, and the globalization of the sport all present tremendous prospects. Cricket has the power to bring people together, to disprove stereotypes, and to raise attention to important social issues.

Cricket, on the other hand, is not without its problems, which include commercialization, inequality, corruption, and the welfare of the players. The delicate balance that must be kept between the commercial interests of the sport and its traditional values must not be disturbed at any cost. The fight against corruption must be steadfast, and inequalities need to be addressed through the implementation of measures that are inclusive.

The governing bodies and leadership of cricket play an important part in determining the course of the sport's future and in fostering societal transformation.

They have the ability to guarantee that cricket will continue to be a driving force behind positive change all across the world if they regulate the sport with transparency, foster an inclusive environment, and put player welfare first.

As aficionados, stakeholders, and fans of cricket, we all have the duty of promoting and upholding the core values that have helped cricket become such a popular sport. We have the ability to collaboratively influence the future of cricket and harness its potential for social change if we accept the opportunities and challenges that lie ahead of us. Cricket has the power to unite disparate communities and promote a better world through the spirit of the game.

8.1 Emerging trends and innovations in Indian cricket

In India, playing cricket is more than simply a pastime—it's a way of life. The sport, which has a devoted following and a long history that dates back to the 18th century, has undergone substantial development in the nation over the course of so many years. From the days when they dominated in test matches to the current era of Twenty20 extravagance, Indian cricket has undergone several shifts throughout its history. The sport has and will continue to hold the nation's attention, and during the past several years, a number of developing tendencies and innovations have radically altered the character of Indian cricket.

The Ascent of Twenty-Twenty Cricket:

The development of Twenty20 (Twenty20) cricket has been one of the most notable trends in Indian cricket in recent years. The Indian Premier League (IPL), which began play in 2008, marked the beginning of a sporting renaissance in India. The Indian Premier League (IPL) established a shorter and more dynamic style of the game, which attracted spectators who may not have been interested in the longer formats of cricket such as test cricket and one-day international cricket (ODI). Because of this innovation, new and aspiring cricket players now have a stage upon which they may demonstrate their skills and earn big salaries.

The Indian Premier League has amassed a significant following not just in India but also in countries all over the world outside of that country. It has resulted in the emergence of new talents, created lucrative chances for players, and altered the way cricket is played and consumed in India. In addition, it has led to the creation of new opportunities. In addition, it is clear that Twenty20 cricket has had a significant impact on the Indian cricket team, as seen by the fact that players such as Rohit Sharma, Virat Kohli, and Jasprit Bumrah have mastered the ability to adapt to numerous formats.

The Beginning of the Era of Women's Cricket:

There has been a recent upswing in the popularity of women's cricket in India. The Indian women's cricket team has seen a great deal of success in recent years, including participation in the ICC Women's World Cup in 2017. As a result, the team has received a great deal of attention and support. The Board of Control for Cricket in India (BCCI) has been making investments in women's cricket by improving facilities, improving coaching, and increasing financial support for female cricket players.

The Women's International Twenty20 Challenge, also known as the Women's Indian Premier League, is one example of how women's cricket has evolved since its inception. This annual competition welcomes competitors from all around the world, including those from the United States, and serves as a stage on which women can showcase their abilities and increase their profile. Not only has the expansion of women's cricket increased the available pool of talent, but it has also served as an inspiration to a new generation of female cricket players in India.

Recent Developments in Technology:

The sport of cricket has adopted technology in order to improve the overall quality of the game, as well as its fairness and entertainment value. One example of a key innovation is the Decision Review System (DRS), which stands for Decision Review System. For the purpose of reviewing umpiring judgments, it employs ball-tracking and edge-detection technologies. The DRS has brought an additional level of precision and openness to the game.

The spectator experience has been significantly improved as a result of the implementation of spider cam and stump mic. Fans may get an insider's perspective on the game thanks to the Spider cam, which captures breathtaking aerial shots of the action, and the stump mics, which pick up player talks and other on-field noise.

In addition to developments in broadcasting, technological advancements have also been made in the areas of training and analysis. Video analysis tools are made available to players and coaches so that they can critically examine their playing styles and game plans. Wearable technology, such as fitness trackers, is also commonly utilized to monitor players' physical conditions and the amount of labor they put in, which enables better monitoring of their fitness.

Insights that Are Driven by Analytics and Data:

The sport of cricket in India has adopted data analytics in order to make judgments that are better informed. Advanced statistical models and performance analytics are utilized by teams in order to design plans, evaluate the strengths and weaknesses of individual players, and determine the optimal compositions of teams. These insights assist teams in improving their overall performance by allowing them to make decisions based on facts.

Fans of cricket have also profited from the advances that have been driven by data. Fans can have a more in-depth understanding of the game and individual player performances through the use of apps and websites that provide real-time statistics and visuals. Fantasy cricket platforms have capitalized on this trend, allowing fans to interact with the sport on a deeper level by selecting their own fantasy teams based on the statistics of players in the real game.

Programs for Youth Development and Local Communities:

The development of young players and grassroots initiatives have been given high priority in Indian cricket. The initiatives of talent scouting and coaching have been broadened in order to recognize and cultivate young talent beginning at an extremely young age. Aspiring cricket players can receive specialized instruction and use of facilities at a number of schools and academies dedicated to the sport of cricket.

The significance of state-level and age-group events has also grown in recent years. These competitions provide a stage for young players to demonstrate their abilities. The Board of Control for Cricket in India (BCCI) and state cricket associations are contributing to the development of young cricket players by investing in infrastructure and resources. The objective is to guarantee that there will always be talented players available for the Indian cricket squad.

The Importance of Exercise:

The modern game of cricket requires a high level of physical fitness, and Indian cricket has acknowledged the significance of maintaining a healthy body. Players are currently at a higher level of physical fitness and agility than ever before. The Yo-Yo test is a high-intensity interval fitness test that is commonly used to evaluate a player's overall level of physical preparedness. Only those candidates who are physically fit enough to meet the requirements set above will be considered for selection.

Not only has the players' on-field performance been enhanced, but the risk of injuries has also been minimized because to the attention placed on fitness. The number of players injured in Indian cricket has been going down, which has made it possible for key players to participate in important matches.

Psychology of Sports and Mental Training for Athletes:

The mental fortitude required to play cricket is of the utmost importance, and Indian cricket has recently begun to place a greater emphasis on sports psychology and mental fitness. Nowadays, players consult with sports psychologists in order to improve their mental toughness, ability to concentrate, and capacity to deal with pressure. This innovation has been critical in assisting athletes in maintaining high levels of performance and overcoming mental obstacles.

The Role of the Captain in Strategic Thinking:

The captains of the Indian cricket team have become into shrewd strategists. Not only are Virat Kohli and Rohit Sharma two of the best batsmen in the world, but they are also excellent leaders who are very good at thinking strategically. They are responsible for making tactical judgments on the field and contributing to the process of identifying the appropriate player combinations. The importance of the role of the captain to the overall performance of the team has grown in recent years.

Participation from Fans:

The rise of social media and other digital channels has completely altered the way that Indian cricket fans engage with the sport. On social media sites such as Twitter, Instagram, and Facebook, teams and players frequently engage in conversation with fans. Through the sharing of thoughts, the posting of videos, and the holding of live chats, they help the fans feel more engaged to the sport.

Additionally, in-stadium experiences have been improved with the addition of entertainment and activities that interest fans who are attending matches. The BCCI has made efforts to create an environment that is welcoming to fans, and it provides a number of different ticket classifications to accommodate the various preferences of fans.

The commercialization of the event, as well as sponsorship:

The marketing of cricket in India has reached new heights in recent years. The Indian Premier League in particular is a huge financial success, as seen by the large number of sponsorships, brand endorsements, and media rights deals that it secures. Cricketers, particularly those who perform well, can make significant salaries from endorsement deals unrelated to the sport through both cricket and other products.

Women in Administrative Roles in Cricket:

A further development that bodes well for the future of Indian cricket is the growing number of women involved in the game's administrative structures. The Board of Control for Cricket in India (BCCI) has given crucial administration jobs to female candidates. This not only encourages the inclusion of people of different genders, but it also provides new insights and ideas to the management of the game.

Ownership of an IPL Franchise :

Not only is the Indian Premier League (IPL) about cricket, but its franchises have also become a symbol of regional pride and identity.

Because it is based on a franchise concept, cricket has been able to attract high-profile individuals and business conglomerates interested in investing and promoting the sport. The owners of franchises have been instrumental in advancing the sport and providing players with access to facilities that are on par with the best in the world.

Several Variables Influencing Game Play:

The addition of day-night test matches and the testing of varied pitch conditions in domestic cricket have both contributed to the increased level of competition and variety in the sport. This invention helps players improve by exposing them to a variety of obstacles, which is beneficial to their overall development. This not only keeps spectators interested in the sport but also adds excitement and an element of unpredictability to it.

Both diversity and inclusivity are important:

The game of cricket in India is becoming increasingly open and welcoming to a wide range of people. As a result of the sport's expansion beyond its traditional strongholds, athletes from a wide variety of states and regions are now making their mark on the national team. This greater diversity not only increases the pool of available talent but also makes sure that cricket is accessible to a wider range of people in the general community.

Talent Spotting at the Local Level:

Because India is such a large country, there is a wealth of undiscovered talent in the more rural parts of the country. New and innovative talent scouting programs have been established in order to discover and cultivate young potential from areas that are underrepresented. These projects intend to close the talent gap that exists between rural and urban cricket by bringing the sport to underserved areas of the country.

Facilities & Infrastructure That Have Been Improved:

The cricketing facilities in India have undergone significant expansion and improvement. In order to offer athletes a playing environment that is on par with the best in the world, numerous improvements have been made, including the renovation of stadiums and the construction of academies. As a result, player development has improved, and India has become a more desirable location for international tours by sports teams.

More Cricket Played on an International Stage:

India has been participating in an increased number of international cricket matches, both at home and outside from their country. More series, tours, and tournaments have been planned, giving players the opportunity to gain experience and enhance their talents against opponents of a higher caliber than ever before.

Adjusting Oneself to Ever-Changing Circumstances:

The Indian cricket team has established itself as one of the best in the world in responding well to shifting playing conditions. Indian cricket has demonstrated its adaptability and resiliency in the face of adversity, whether it be in the form of changing to foreign pitches or in the form of adapting to biosecure bubbles during the COVID-19 pandemic.

Programs at the Local Level:

Cricket programs at the grassroots level have become increasingly important for the development of new talent. Young cricketers are being discovered and developed via youth programs at schools, academies, and state levels beginning at a very young age. This helps to ensure that there will be a consistent supply of talented players in the years to come.

Women in Radio, Television, and Print Commentary:

A further development that is worthy of note is the growing number of women working in broadcasting and commentary jobs. Women experts and commentators are bringing a novel viewpoint on the sport, and their observations and evaluations are assisting in the process of expanding the cricketing discourse in the country.

The expansion of domestic Twenty20 leagues:

Domestic Twenty20 tournaments like the Syed Mushtaq Ali Trophy and the Vijay Hazare Trophy have gained significance in recent years alongside the Indian Premier League (IPL). These competitions not only give domestic players a stage on which to exhibit their skills, but also act as a source of potential players for both the Indian Premier League and the Indian national team.

An Increase in the Participation of Fans:

Fans are now able to participate in a more engaging manner, thanks to the proliferation of social media and digital platforms. Their experience of watching cricket may be made more immersive by allowing them to vote for their favorite players, make predictions about the outcomes of matches, and engage in conversations with other fans.

Initiatives Concerning the Environment and Sustainability:

In addition, Indian cricket has demonstrated its dedication to sustainable practices and responsible stewardship of the environment. The utilization of solar electricity, rainwater harvesting, and waste management methods are just some of the green efforts that stadiums are rapidly incorporating into their operations in order to become more environmentally friendly.

How Coaching Has Changed Over Time:

The methods of coaching have undergone substantial development in India. The utilization of sophisticated coaching techniques, the incorporation of technology, as well as the involvement of international coaches, have all contributed to an improvement in the overall quality of player development and coaching.

Expanding Our Scope Around the World:

The global influence of Indian cricket is extending beyond the confines of the cricket field. The administrators, coaches, and players of Indian cricket are making important contributions to the expansion and development of the sport of cricket around the world. On the international scene, they participate in a variety of cricket-related activities, including mentoring other teams, exchanging information, and mentoring, and sharing knowledge.

Innovations that Focus on the Fans:

Several improvements that focus on the fan experience have been implemented recently in order to improve it. This includes interactive smartphone apps, experiences in virtual reality, and in-stadium technologies that let fans to participate with the game in novel ways.

Fantasy cricket and electronic sports:

E-sports and fantasy cricket have been increasingly popular in recent years, which has introduced a new facet to fan participation. E-sports events that are based on cricket games and fantasy cricket platforms have gained an enormous amount of popularity in recent years. These tournaments give fans the opportunity to not only watch the sport but also take part in it in a virtual form.

Increasing Numbers of Females Participating in Twenty20 Cricket:

The Women's T20 Challenge, which is held concurrently with the Indian Premier League (IPL), has gained popularity and has begun to highlight the extraordinary ability of female cricket players. Women's cricket is receiving increased attention and investment, which has contributed to the sport's growing popularity.

Adoption of Technology at the Grassroots:

Even at the most fundamental levels, technological solutions are being implemented to improve coaching and talent scouting. In order to foster the development of youthful talent, video analysis tools, performance tracking apps, and online coaching resources are being utilized.

Initiatives that Focus on the Fans:

Initiatives like as "Cricket for All" have been created in order to make the sport more approachable and pleasant for its followers. The goal of these programs is to broaden the appeal of cricket by reaching out to spectators in rural and economically disadvantaged areas.

8.2 Potential areas for further social impact

It is essential that, as we traverse the intricacies of the 21st century, we recognize that addressing societal concerns and promoting human well-being involves continuous innovation and investment in a variety of fields. This realization is especially important given the fact that the 21st century is already well underway. There are an infinite number of fields in which additional societal influence can be made, ranging from medicine and science to education and the protection of natural resources. During this talk, we will examine eight potential areas for additional social impact, with a focus on the significance of ongoing growth and change in order to build a better future.

Renewable sources of energy and environmentally responsible practices:

The continual transition around the world toward sustainable practices and renewable sources of energy is an essential component for increased social impact. The Earth is in considerable danger from the effects of climate change, pollution, and the depletion of resources. Investing in renewable energy sources like solar, wind, and hydroelectric power can help reduce emissions of greenhouse gases and foster a more sustainable energy future. Furthermore, the implementation of sustainable practices in agricultural operations, industrial practices, and transportation practices can help alleviate the harm done to the environment and build a society that is cleaner and healthier for future generations.

Equity in Healthcare Provision and Access

Enhancing both accessibility and equity in medical treatment is a topic with enormous potential for positive societal effect. Many people in different parts of the world do not have access to fundamental medical services, which results in illnesses and deaths that could have been avoided. The expansion of inexpensive healthcare services, the improvement of healthcare infrastructure in neglected locations, and the reduction of healthcare inequities are all potential initiatives that can be taken to address this issue. Communities that are geographically isolated or otherwise underserved may benefit greatly from the use of telemedicine and other digital health platforms to expand their access to medical care.

Education & Learning Throughout One's Life:

Putting money into schools and programs that encourage ongoing education can have a significant positive effect on entire cultures. Not only is the right to an education of sufficient quality an essential component of human dignity, but it is also one of the most effective means of breaking the vicious cycle of poverty.

Education may become more democratic and open to people of all ages and walks of life if technological advancements in the field of education were to take place, such as the development of online learning platforms. Education in the STEM fields (Science, Technology, Engineering, and Mathematics), vocational training, and the development of skills are all ways in which individuals might be better prepared for the dynamic labor market.

Support and Education Regarding Mental Health:

In recent years, there has been a growing awareness that mental health is an essential component of overall wellbeing. However, individuals are still discouraged from getting help when they require it due to the stigma associated with the issue as well as a lack of available services. Increasing awareness about mental health concerns, developing communities that are welcoming and supportive of one another, and making certain that mental health services are not only available but also reasonably priced are all necessary steps toward expanding social impact in this area. Additionally, developments in teletherapy and smartphone applications for mental health are making it simpler for individuals to have access to available resources and support.

Justice for all and respect for human rights:

In a society where injustice and discrimination still exist, promoting social justice and human rights is a continuing task. This is especially true in the United States. In order to advance social effect in this area, it is necessary to eradicate systemic inequalities, advocate for communities that are on the margins, and press for legal reforms. Continued focus and action are required to address pressing issues such as racial equality, gender equity, LGBTQ+ rights, and refugee protection.

Preparedness for Emergencies and Emergency Response:

Natural disasters are occurring with greater regularity and severity, and global health crises, such as pandemics, are also on the rise, all of which underscore the need for increased social impact in emergency preparedness and response. Putting money into early warning systems, catastrophe resilience, and quick emergency response mechanisms has the potential to both save lives and reduce the severity of damage. Additionally, medical research, vaccine development, and global health initiatives play a key part in preparing for and responding to health disasters.

Agriculture that is sustainable and ensuring adequate food supply:

It is a big problem to provide food for the world's ever-increasing population while also reducing agriculture's negative effects on the environment. Food production can have a smaller carbon footprint if sustainable agricultural practices such as organic farming, precision farming, and agroforestry are implemented.

In addition, ensuring food security by doing away with hunger, decreasing the amount of food wasted, and broadening access to food that is high in nutrients is crucial to achieving a more fair and sustainable future.

Community Development and Participation in Civic Life:

The power of communities and their engaged participation in the decision-making processes at the local, national, and international levels are very necessary in order to bring about constructive social change. It is possible for initiatives to achieve social effect if they promote community building, civic education, and active engagement in democratic processes. It is possible to empower individuals and build social cohesion by encouraging community-led development projects, grassroots organizing, and volunteerism at the community level.

8.3 The role of cricket in India's evolving society

Cricket is more than simply a sport to the people of India; it has evolved into an essential component of the cultural landscape of the nation as a whole throughout the course of its lengthy history as a national pastime. It is more than simply a game; it is a unifying force that draws people together from a wide variety of cultural and linguistic origins as well as geographical locations. Cricket has, over the course of its history, been an important factor in the development of India's society, helping to contribute to the nation's sense of identity, social cohesiveness, and international recognition. The sport has knitted itself into the social, cultural, and economic fabric of India in a variety of different ways, ranging from its historical significance to its modern impact on the country.

The Integration of Cultures:

Cricket has been a potent driver of cultural unification in India throughout the course of its long history. It fosters a sense of shared identity and pride among people from different states, languages, and cultural backgrounds, uniting them around a common cause. When the Indian cricket team competes, millions of people from all walks of life come together to show their support for the team and celebrate its successes, fostering a sense of national togetherness and solidarity.

Characterizing a Nation:

Cricket is often credited with significantly contributing to the formation and maturation of India's sense of national identity. The country's achievements on the cricket field have frequently been seen as symbolic victories, representing the nation's resiliency and commitment in its pursuit of its goals. The Indian mindset has been permanently altered by momentous victories, like as the 1983 Cricket World Cup and the 2007 T20 World Cup, which have instilled a sense of national pride and accomplishment.

Aspiration and Opportunities for Social Mobility:

The sport of cricket has been used as a means of social mobility, providing a route to achievement for people who come from less privileged beginnings. Many prominent cricketers who have risen to popularity over the years, such as MS Dhoni, Sachin Tendulkar, and Virat Kohli, have become role models for millions of young people around the country who are interested in playing cricket. Their rise from humble beginnings to global prominence has motivated an entire generation to chase after their ambitions and achieve the best that they are capable of.

Influence on the Economy:

The sport of cricket has a large and positive effect on India's economy. The sport brings in a substantial amount of money from a variety of different avenues of revenue generation, such as television rights, sponsorships, retail sales, and ticket sales. In example, the Indian Premier League (IPL) has developed into a lucrative platform, which has attracted investments from a variety of enterprises both in India and around the world. Because of this economic impact, the sports business has expanded, and as a result, infrastructure and facilities relating to cricket have been developed all throughout the country.

Maintaining Social Cohesion:

Cricket has been instrumental in bringing people closer together and enhancing their sense of camaraderie over the course of its history. It acts as a meeting place for people of varying socioeconomic situations, who all have a common interest in cheering on their favorite teams and players. Cricket has the capacity to foster a sense of connection and community spirit among its fans, whether that be by rooting for local teams competing in domestic leagues or supporting the national team competing in international events.

The Empowerment of Women :

Women's cricket in India is receiving a rising amount of recognition and support, both of which have helped to the empowerment of women in sports. The accomplishments of the Indian women's cricket team on the world scene, in conjunction with events such as the Women's Indian Premier League, have inspired an increased number of young women to pursue professional careers in cricket. Women cricketers have been able to challenge traditional gender conventions and have helped pave the road for greater gender equality in Indian culture as a result of their increased exposure and recognition in the sport.

Motivating Factors: Inspiration and Aspiration

Millions of young people in India have looked to cricket as a source of motivation and an avenue toward achieving their goals. A new generation has been encouraged to consider a career in sports as a result of the exploits of cricketing icons.

This has led to the professionalization of cricket as well as the establishment of organized training programs and academies all throughout the country. Young people have been inspired with optimism and ambition by the achievements of cricket players, which has motivated them to pursue excellence in the sectors that they have chosen to pursue.

Programming for Young People:

Cricket has been an extremely important factor in the growth and development of young people in India, helping to teach in them virtues such as perseverance, sportsmanship, collaboration, and discipline. Young athletes have the opportunity to demonstrate their skills and develop their passion for the game thanks to the platform that the sport gives. Cricket is a sport that has seen increased engagement from younger generations as a result of grassroots programs, coaching initiatives, and inter-school championships. These activities have helped to foster overall growth and character development in the younger generation.

The Media and the Entertainment Industry:

The sport's influence on Indian culture has been further increased as a result of the mutually beneficial relationship that exists between cricket, the media, and entertainment. A robust cricket ecosystem has been formed as a result of extensive coverage of cricket matches, pre-match analysis, post-match conversations, and cricket-related entertainment shows. This has attracted the attention of millions of fans across the country. The integration of cricket into many forms of media and entertainment has helped to contribute to the sport's meteoric rise in popularity as well as its growing cultural importance.

Recognizance on a Global Scale:

The accomplishments of India's cricket team have won praise and admiration from cricket fans all across the world. The rise of the nation to the position of preeminent power in international cricket has resulted in an increase in both its worldwide standing and its impact in the field of sports. India has established itself as a force in the world of cricket thanks to its successes in international tournaments and the popularity of the Indian Premier League (IPL). As a result, cricket fans all over the world are paying attention to India and admiring their achievements.

Chapter 9

Conclusion

Cricket, known as the "gentleman's game," has moved beyond its traditional limitations as a sport and developed into a potent agent of social change in India. In the course of this in-depth investigation, we have gone deeply into the myriad of roles that cricket plays in India, as well as its historical setting and the profound effect that the sport has had on the evolution of society. Cricket has developed into more than simply a game; it is a symbol of unification, an engine for social development, and a source of inspiration for generations to come. During the colonial era, cricket was a sport played by the elite; today, it is a nationwide passion that grabs the hearts of millions.

The incredible journey that cricket has taken as a catalyst for social transformation in India is a testament to the sport's everlasting relevance and influence. Throughout the course of this voyage, several fundamental themes have surfaced, highlighting the significant effects that the sport has had on a variety of facets of Indian society.

Integration of Culture and the Formation of National Identity:

In spite of language, geographical, and cultural divides, cricket has succeeded in bringing a varied nation together. It has helped to cultivate a sense of national identity by bringing together millions of people of all origins in India under the common purpose of cheering on their favorite teams. The integration of culture that has been brought about by cricket extends far beyond the realm of the sport itself, permeating people's everyday lives and the conversations they have. The successes of the Indian cricket team have been recognized not only as athletic accomplishments but also as defining events for the pride of the nation.

The Impact on the Economy, and Professionalization:

There is no denying the positive effect that cricket has had on India's economy. The sector that revolves around the sport has grown to be worth several billions of dollars thanks to the success of television, sponsorships, merchandise, and ticket sales at stadiums. The Indian Premier League (IPL) is a monument to the economic power of cricket, as it has been successful in luring investments from business giants and independent business owners. This financial heft has resulted in the professionalization of the sport, and cricketers today enjoy rich careers; as a result, cricket has become an appealing choice for young athletes wanting to pursue a career in sports.

Aspiration and Opportunities for Social Mobility:

The stories of countless cricketers who have risen from humble beginnings to achieve international stardom are illustrative of the democratizing effect that cricket has had on the sport. Their travels, which are frequently fraught with obstacles and difficulties, serve as a source of motivation and aspiration for millions of young people living in India. The sport has provided talented people with a route to achievement that is not limited by the conventional barriers of caste, class, or socioeconomic standing. These barriers have been broken down as a result of the sport.

Developing Young People and Strengthening Their Character:

The sport of cricket has been instrumental in molding the personalities of India's younger generation. It teaches the importance of discipline, working together as a team, not giving up, and having good sportsmanship. The sport offers a stage upon which young athletes can demonstrate their potential and pursue their interests. Youth engagement in cricket has been encouraged thanks to grassroots programs, coaching efforts, and inter-school competitions. These events provide a place for the all-around growth and cultivation of skills in young people.

The Empowerment of Women :

Long neglected, the sport of women's cricket in India has recently experienced a stunning renaissance. Together with other efforts, such as the Women's Indian Premier League, the successes of the Indian women's cricket team on the world stage have contributed to the empowerment of women in sports. The attention and acknowledgement given to female cricketers has helped to defy gender conventions, which has contributed to the development of a more egalitarian society and encouraged more women to get involved in sports.

Nexus of the Media and the Entertainment Industry:

The sport's influence on Indian culture has been magnified as a result of the symbiotic relationship that exists between cricket, the media, and entertainment. A flourishing ecosystem has been formed around the sport of cricket as a result of extensive coverage of cricket matches, pre-match analysis, post-match conversations, and cricket-related entertainment programs. Cricket has surpassed the limitations of a mere game to become a cultural phenomenon, capturing the interest and imagination of millions upon millions of fans all over the world.

Building Community and Promoting Social Cohesion:

By bringing people from all different walks of life together, cricket has contributed to the growth of social cohesion. Cricket fosters a sense of belonging and community spirit among its fans, whether they are rooting for their country in international competitions or showing support for their neighborhood clubs in domestic leagues.

The sense of community that exists among cricket fans cuts over socioeconomic lines, geographic boundaries, and language barriers, all of which contribute to the development of a more harmonious society.

The story of how cricket came to play such an important part in India's rapidly changing society is one of dedication, tenacity, and evolution. Not only has it acted as a mirror that reflects the journey that the nation has taken, but it has also actively contributed to determining the direction that it has taken. Cricket is more than simply a sport; it is a mirror of a robust and diverse society, a bridge that links millions of people, and an expression of ambitions and aspirations.

The game of cricket in India is a great example of the potential for sports to be a driving force behind social transformation. It has inspired individuals to rise above obstacles and strive for excellence, which has the effect of uniting a nation that is diverse and complex. The importance of cricket's role in molding India's future has not diminished, even as the sport continues to develop and adapt to new circumstances. In the years to ahead, future generations will continue to be influenced by the sport's long legacy as a symbol of unity, inspiration, and aspiration. This will help to develop a society that is more inclusive, equal, and peaceful. In India, cricket is more than simply a sport; it is a way of life, a source of optimism, and a connector that brings together a nation with over a billion different goals.

9.1 Recap of cricket's transformative role in Indian society

Cricket, which is commonly referred to as the "gentleman's game," has had an extremely significant impact on the culture and civilization of India. It's more than just a game; it's a cultural phenomenon, a wellspring of creativity, and a window into India's constantly shifting sense of who it is. During the course of this in-depth investigation, we were able to decipher the complexities of cricket's transformative role in Indian culture by tracking its historical path, sociocultural impact, and profound consequences on a variety of facets of life in India.

This review serves as a comprehensive summary of the primary ideas and insights that were discussed throughout the course of this conversation. It also aims to emphasize the transforming function that cricket plays in Indian society.

Contextualization historique:

The sport of cricket didn't have its start in India until the colonial era, when the British first brought it over from England. At first, it was a sport that was predominantly performed by members of higher social classes, and it was connected to those who held positions of authority. Nevertheless, over the course of time, it was able to overcome these limitations and find its way into the hearts of everyday Indians.

During the fight for independence, cricket matches evolved into platforms on which political and social opinions could be voiced. As a result, the sport came to be seen as a symbol of resistance.

Integration of Culture and the Formation of National Identity:

In India, cricket has served as a unifying factor, bringing together individuals whose linguistic, regional, and cultural roots are vastly different from one another. It encourages a feeling of national identity by bringing together millions of people of different backgrounds in India under the common goal of cheering on their favorite teams. The triumphs of the Indian cricket team are occasions worthy of celebration since they serve as defining moments for the pride and unity of the nation.

The Impact on the Economy, and Professionalization:

The sport of cricket has had a significant impact on India's economy. As a result of revenue streams coming from television rights, sponsorships, item sales, and ticket sales, it has grown into an industry worth several billions of dollars. The Indian Premier League (IPL) is a monument to the economic power of cricket, as it has been successful in luring investments from business giants and independent business owners. This economic influence has resulted in the professionalization of the sport, elevating cricket to the status of a desirable career option for prospective athletes.

Aspiration and Opportunities for Social Mobility:

The role that cricket plays in the process of social mobility is one of the most impressive aspects of its impact. A multitude of cricketers have climbed from modest beginnings to achieve international stardom, serving as role models for millions of young people throughout India. The sport has provided talented people with a route to achievement that is not limited by the conventional barriers of caste, class, or socio-economic standing. These barriers have been broken down as a result of the sport. The lives of cricket players like MS Dhoni, Sachin Tendulkar, and Virat Kohli are living proof that the sport has the capacity to transcend socio-economic divides.

Developing Young People and Strengthening Their Character:

The sport of cricket has been instrumental in molding the personalities of India's younger generation. It teaches the importance of discipline, working together as a team, not giving up, and having good sportsmanship. The sport offers a stage upon which young athletes can demonstrate their potential and pursue their interests. Youth participation in cricket has been encouraged thanks to grass-roots programs, coaching efforts, and inter-school contests. These activities all contribute to holistic development and the cultivation of abilities.

The Empowerment of Women :

Long neglected, the sport of women's cricket in India has recently experienced a stunning renaissance. Together with other efforts, such as the Women's Indian Premier League, the successes of the Indian women's cricket team on the world stage have contributed to the empowerment of women in sports. The attention and acknowledgement given to female cricketers has helped to defy gender conventions, which has contributed to the development of a more egalitarian society and encouraged more women to get involved in sports.

Nexus of the Media and the Entertainment Industry:

The sport's influence on Indian culture has been magnified as a result of the symbiotic relationship that exists between cricket, the media, and entertainment. A flourishing ecosystem has been formed around the sport of cricket as a result of extensive coverage of cricket matches, pre-match analysis, post-match conversations, and cricket-related entertainment programs. Cricket has surpassed the limitations of a mere game to become a cultural phenomenon, capturing the interest and imagination of millions upon millions of fans all over the world.

Building Community and Promoting Social Cohesion:

By bringing people from all different walks of life together, cricket has contributed to the growth of social cohesion. Cricket fosters a sense of belonging and community spirit among its fans, whether they are rooting for their country in international competitions or showing support for their neighborhood clubs in domestic leagues. The sense of community that exists among cricket fans cuts over socioeconomic lines, geographic boundaries, and language barriers, all of which contribute to the development of a more harmonious society.

The story of how cricket came to play such an important part in India's rapidly changing society is one of dedication, tenacity, and evolution. Not only has it acted as a mirror that reflects the journey that the nation has taken, but it has also actively contributed to determining the direction that it has taken. Cricket is more than simply a sport; it is a mirror of a robust and diverse society, a bridge that links millions of people, and an expression of ambitions and aspirations.

As we review the significant role that cricket has played in the evolution of Indian culture, it becomes clear that the influence of the sport reaches well beyond the confines of a single cricket stadium. Because of its ability to bring people together, serve as an inspiration, and dismantle barriers, it has become an essential component of India's cultural fabric. The importance of cricket's role in molding India's future has not diminished, even as the sport continues to develop and adapt to new circumstances. In the years to ahead, future generations will continue to be influenced by the sport's long legacy as a symbol of unity, inspiration, and aspiration.

This will help to develop a society that is more inclusive, equal, and peaceful. In India, cricket is more than simply a sport; it is a way of life, a source of optimism, and a connector that brings together a nation with over a billion different goals.

9.2 The enduring importance of cricket in shaping India's future

Cricket, which is frequently referred to as the "religion" of India, has had an enduring impact on the social landscape, cultural landscape, and economic landscape of the country. Beyond the area of merely being a sport, cricket occupies a special place in the hearts of millions of people, acting as a unifying force, a source of inspiration, and a symbol of national pride in countries all over the world. It is impossible to overestimate the significance of this factor in determining India's destiny. In the course of this in-depth investigation, we will look into the continuing relevance of cricket and the ways in which it continues to play a key role in molding the future of India.

Importance in the Course of History:

The development of cricket in India is intricately entwined with the country's long and illustrious history. Cricket was once considered a sport for members of higher social classes when it was first played after its introduction by the British during the colonial era. However, its development over the course of the years is a reflection of the changes that have taken place within Indian society. Cricket, which served as a venue for political and social manifestations of resistance against colonial rule, played an important part in India's fight for independence and was an important part of the conflict. The significance of this event in the nation's history provided the groundwork for cricket's ongoing role in the formation of the nation's identity and the future.

Integration of Culture and the Formation of National Identity:

Cricket has been an extremely important factor in the development of a sense of national identity and cohesion in India. The sport is able to bridge linguistic, regional, and cultural divides, and as a result, it attracts participants from a wide variety of backgrounds. When the Indian cricket team competes, millions of people from all walks of life come together to show their support and celebrate the team's successes. Cricket is more than simply a sport; it's an experience that brings people together and gives them a sense that they are part of a broader Indian community.

It is clear that cricket will continue to play an important role in the development of India's future because of its capacity to bring people of different communities together and instill in them a feeling of shared identity. It acts as a force that brings people together, which in turn helps to reinforce the nation's social fabric.

The Impact on the Economy, and Professionalization:

The sport of cricket has a significant impact on India's economy. It has developed into an industry that is worth several billions of dollars, with cash coming in from television rights, sponsorships, retail sales, and ticket sales. Specifically, the Indian Premier League (IPL) has become a financial powerhouse, drawing investments from companies both in India and beyond the world. The sport's growing influence in the global economy has elevated cricket to the level of a profession, opening up rich opportunities for its players. As the industry surrounding cricket continues to flourish, it presents cricket players with a number of exciting career prospects and makes a substantial contribution to the expansion of the nation's economy.

The potential of cricket to both offer economic opportunities and elevate itself to the level of a professional sport is another evidence of the sport's continuing significance. Not only does it provide players with a means of subsistence, but it also bolsters a wide range of ancillary sectors, from the media to the hospitality industry, so helping to the growth of India's economy.

Aspiration and Opportunities for Social Mobility:

Cricket's significance as a vehicle for social advancement has proven to be one of the sport's most enduring impacts. People who come from less fortunate circumstances have the opportunity to climb the ranks of their sport and achieve success and recognition. Cricketers like MS Dhoni, Sachin Tendulkar, and Virat Kohli, who came from relatively unimportant places but have now achieved international acclaim, serve as a source of motivation for tens of millions of impressionable young people in India. Their experiences demonstrate the power of cricket to break down socioeconomic barriers and open doors for aspiring players, and serve as a tribute to the power of cricket.

The power of cricket to inspire and drive younger people is one of the reasons it will always be important in the process of determining India's future. In the eyes of innumerable young people, the stories of cricket players who have beaten the obstacles and reached the summit of their sport instill hope and desire, motivating them to follow their goals of playing the sport professionally.

Developing Young People and Strengthening Their Character:

The game of cricket has been extremely important to the growth and development of young people in India. Discipline, perseverance, collaboration, and sportsmanship are all taught through participation in the sport. Cricket is a sport that helps young people acquire important life skills while also teaching them the technical parts of the game. Youth participation in cricket has been increased thanks to grassroots programs, coaching initiatives, and inter-school contests. Cricket serves as a platform for the holistic growth and character development of its participants.

It is clear that cricket will continue to play a significant part in the development of future leaders in India because of the function it plays in the development of youthful talent. The sport teaches young people vital abilities and characteristics that may be applied to areas of life other than playing cricket, so preparing them to be successful in a variety of facets of life.

The Empowerment of Women :

In recent years in India, women's cricket has been receiving a growing amount of notice as well as support. Together with other efforts, such as the Women's Indian Premier League, the successes of the Indian women's cricket team on the world stage have contributed to the empowerment of women in sports. The visibility and acknowledgement of women cricketers presents a challenge to the conventional gender norms that exist in Indian society and helps advance the cause of gender equality.

The empowerment of women is one of the many ways that cricket will continue to play an important role in India's future. It does this by providing opportunities for leadership and overcoming gender stereotypes while encouraging young women to explore their interests in sports.

Nexus of the Media and the Entertainment Industry:

Cricket, the media, and entertainment all have a complicated and everlasting relationship with one another. A robust ecosystem has developed around the sport of cricket as a result of extensive coverage of cricket matches, as well as pre-match analysis, post-match conversations, and cricket-related entertainment programs. Cricket has developed into a cultural phenomenon, capturing the attention and imagination of a huge number of people all over the world. It is no longer simply a game.

The ability of cricket to foster the growth of India's entertainment industry is evidence of the sport's enduring significance in the process of reshaping India's future. People are compelled to participate, there is a venue for the transmission of oral history, and it is a source of enjoyment that has an impact on Indian society and culture.

Building Community and Promoting Social Cohesion:

Cricket has been an important force in the country of India's efforts to strengthen social cohesiveness. It brings together people from all kinds of different backgrounds, generating a sense of community and belonging in those who participate. Fans of cricket have a connection that is unaffected by socioeconomic status, location, or language barriers, as evidenced by the fact that they can be found all over the world rooting for their respective national teams in international competitions as well as in domestic leagues.

The capacity of cricket to foster inclusive societies is illustrative of the game's enduring significance in the process of reshaping India's future. It fosters social cohesiveness and contributes to the strengthening of the social fabric of the nation, so establishing a sense of oneness among the many different communities.

It is a monument to the sport's long heritage and significance that cricket will continue to play an important role in the development of India's future. Cricket has not only acted as a mirror that reflects the journey that the nation has taken but has also actively helped to defining the course that it has taken. The importance of cricket's role in molding India's future has not diminished, even as the sport continues to develop and adapt to new circumstances.

In India, cricket is more than simply a sport; it is a way of life, a source of optimism, and a connector that brings together a nation with over a billion different goals. In the years to come, it will continue to contribute to the growth of a society that is more welcoming, equal, and harmonious by virtue of its capacity to bring people together, to inspire them, and to effect transformation. The history of cricket will continue to have a profound impact on India's future, acting as a unifying force and a source of inspiration and aspiration. It is a power that can be traced back through the ages, permanently imprinting itself on the collective consciousness of the nation.

9.3 Final thoughts on the potential for cricket to drive social change in India

Cricket, which is sometimes lauded as the heart and soul of India, has shown an incredible ability to promote societal transformation in the country. [Cricket is] commonly regarded as India's national pastime. This conversation has taken a comprehensive look at the myriad ways in which cricket has impacted Indian society, including its historical significance, its part in the formation of cultural identity, its influence on the economy, its role in the empowerment of women, and its contribution to the formation of communities. As we come to the end of this in-depth investigation, it is of the utmost importance to ruminate on the potential of cricket to further propel social transformation in India.

The transforming influence of cricket in India stretches well beyond the confines of cricket stadiums and fields. It is a force that transcends linguistic, geographical, and cultural barriers in order to unite a nation that is culturally, regionally, and linguistically varied. The sport is profoundly established in the collective consciousness of the people of India, becoming a shared experience that contributes to the development of a sense of belonging to a broader community. Because of this oneness, which was spurred on by cricket, there is a chance for social transformation in many other facets of Indian society.

Encouraging Inclusion and Equal Opportunity:

Cricket has the ability to foster inclusivity and equality in India, and this country should take advantage of this. People from many walks of life can find common ground via their shared love of a particular sport and its teams and players, which serves as a unifying force. These fleeting moments of cohesion have the potential to be used to create tolerance and acceptance of differences, so contributing to the development of a society that is more inclusive. Cricket has the potential to act as a catalyst for change in India by removing barriers relating to caste, class, and religion, so demonstrating how India can become more egalitarian.

Education and the Personal Growth of Young People:

The empowerment of young people is one of the most important ways in which cricket can propel social change. For the purpose of fostering young talent and developing good character, grassroots programs, coaching efforts, and competitions amongst schools are absolutely necessary. The younger generation may benefit from having the characteristics of discipline, collaboration, perseverance, and sportsmanship instilled in them through participation in cricket. In addition, the sport has the potential to play a significant part in advancing education and drawing attention to the significance of academics in addition to athletics. Young cricketers have a lot to gain from opportunities like scholarships, mentorship programs, and educational incentives. These can help pave the road for a better future for many people.

The Empowerment of Women :

The cricket experience can have a transforming effect on women, which has the ability to unleash tremendous potential. The achievements of the Indian women's cricket team have pushed the boundaries of conventional gender stereotypes and served as a source of motivation for young women all around the country. By challenging traditional gender roles and opening doors for women to participate in sports and leadership positions, fostering and encouraging women's cricket has the potential to be a socially transformative force. It is possible for initiatives in the sport of cricket to have a ripple impact on gender equality in other aspects of society if they give women with equal access, resources, and recognition.

Responsibility to one's community and charitable giving:

Cricketing icons and organizations have the potential to utilize their influence to propel positive social change through the pursuit of charitable activities. The cricketing community, which includes players, franchises, and regulatory bodies, has the potential to engage in charitable work and make a positive contribution to society as a whole. Underserved communities have the potential to be positively impacted for the long term by actions taken in the areas of healthcare, education, environmental protection, and disaster assistance. Cricketers have the potential to serve as models for social responsibility, thereby motivating spectators to make contributions to organizations that matter.

Building Community and Promoting Social Cohesion:

The great ability of cricket to encourage social bonding and community building makes it an effective instrument for bringing about social change. The sense of community that exists among cricket fans, whether they follow their favorite local clubs or the national team, is a resource that may be utilized to find solutions to societal problems. These communities have the potential to collaborate in order to address issues such as inequality in education and employment rates as well as poverty. They have the potential to act as support networks, allowing individuals to overcome obstacles and flourish as a result.

Becoming Aware of Mental Health:

The topic of athletes' mental health has received an increasing amount of attention in recent years. Because of the sport's enormous fan base, cricket has the ability to normalize conversations about mental health and reduce the associated stigma. The cricketing community has the opportunity to actively participate in conversations on mental health, to share personal experiences, and to urge others to get help when they require it. Cricket has the potential to be a social force for change by decreasing the stigma that is connected with mental health issues. This can be accomplished by openly discussing issues related to mental health.

Sustainability in Relation to the Environment:

The cricket has the potential to be a driving force behind more sustainable environmental practices. The construction and upkeep of cricket stadiums, in addition to the substantial traveling that is required for international cricket, have environmental repercussions. Cricket has the potential to serve as a model for the conservation of natural resources if it were to implement environmentally responsible policies and procedures, such as the utilization of renewable energy sources, the construction of sustainable stadiums, and the management of waste. It has the potential to increase eco-awareness among players and fans, thereby driving social change in the direction of a greener future.

Educational Programs and Professional Capability Building:

Cricket has the potential to significantly contribute to the advancement of educational programs and professional capabilities. The game has the potential to encourage young people to prioritize their studies alongside their cricket careers. Opportunities to acquire important life skills can be made available to aspiring young cricketers through things like scholarships, mentoring programs, and vocational training. These programs have the potential to not only improve their quality of life but also to make a contribution to the overall growth and development of the country's young people.

There is a tremendous and significant amount of potential for cricket to drive social transformation in India.

It is a force that extends well beyond the confines of a game, motivating individuals from different parts of the country to cooperate in order to achieve common objectives. Because of the sport's impact on cultural integration, empowerment, inclusivity, and social cohesion, the groundwork has been created for a future in which cricket can be utilized as an effective instrument for bringing about positive change. The most important step is to first acknowledge that cricket has the potential to be a force for social change, and then take active steps to realize that promise.

Cricket has the power to bring people together, to inspire them, and to change them. The cricketing community and society in general may create social change that resonates far beyond the cricket field by capitalizing on the impact that the cricketing community possesses. Because of its continuing significance in determining India's future, cricket will continue to play an essential part in the development of a society that is more welcoming, equal, and peaceful. As cricket develops, so is the possibility that it will bring about societal transformation. This will leave an indelible stamp on the collective path of the nation.